DATE DUE

F
251
.D83

Nuermberger, Ruth Anna
(Ketring)

The free produce movement

JAN 1977

MAR '89

AUG 1980   SEP 83

7687

Historical Papers of the
Trinity College Historical Society
Series XXV

THE FREE PRODUCE MOVEMENT

A Quaker Protest Against Slavery

BY

RUTH KETRING NUERMBERGER

1942

AMS PRESS
New York

COPYRIGHT © 1942, DUKE UNIVERSITY PRESS

Reprinted with permission
First AMS EDITION published 1970
Manufactured in the United States of America

SBN: complete set: 404-51750-1
volume 25: 404-51775-7

Library of Congress Catalog Card Number: 73-110135

AMS PRESS, INC.
NEW YORK, N. Y. 10003

To
ANNA COX BRINTON
Decori decus addit avito

PREFACE

This history of the free produce movement is the result of investigations carried on over a period of several years. The free produce movement was essentially an organized effort to boycott goods produced by slave labor. As a means to advance the abolition of slavery it had only limited success.

The subject was first encountered by the writer when she was preparing, as an M.A. thesis, a biography of Charles Osborn, who was one of the leaders in the free produce movement. The curiosity aroused by that first contact with this obscure reform effort has led to the present result.

The movement was sponsored chiefly by the Society of Friends, most of them plain, unpretentious people, whose work made no mark in national annals. Many of them left no records which have been preserved, while the great body of abolition literature generally contains no information on the free produce movement. Although supported chiefly by Quakers, the free produce cause was never officially sponsored, and scarcely sanctioned, by the Society of Friends as a religious organization. While many prominent abolitionists endorsed the boycott idea, they did not advocate it publicly as a means of combating slavery.

Sources for the study of this almost unknown phase of the abolition movement are few and scattered. Bibliographies and indices yield almost no information. Hence the discovery of much of the material herein cited has been lucky accident. For years the writer despaired of achieving a connected story, but time, chance, luck, and assistance from several Quaker historians have resulted in a narrative by no means complete, but at least possessed of continuity.

The existence of the free produce movement seems not to be known to historians generally, and indeed scarcely to those who give their attention to the anti-slavery movement. Only the historians of Quakerism appear to have some knowledge of it. Consequently, where the free produce movement touched the lives of national figures—John Greenleaf Whittier or Gerrit Smith or Harriet Beecher Stowe, for instance—their biographers have ignored the fact, presumably because they did not understand it and no concise explanation was available.

PREFACE

In gathering the material for this study the author has visited some twenty libraries. These include the Bixby Memorial Library of Vergennes, Vermont, the Boston Public Library, the Huntington Library, the Library Company of Philadelphia, and the Library of Congress; the libraries of Brown, Duke, Harvard, Ohio State, and Syracuse universities; of Earlham, Guilford, Haverford, Oberlin, and Swarthmore colleges; the Historical Society of Pennsylvania, Indiana State Library, the Ohio State Archaeological and Historical Society, and the Western Reserve Historical Society. To the staffs of all these institutions the author owes thanks, and especially to Anna B. Hewitt of Haverford and E. Virginia Walker of the Friends' Historical Library at Swarthmore College.

Special acknowledgments go to Francis R. Taylor of Philadelphia, for making available his large manuscript collection covering the movement; to Thomas E. Drake of Haverford, for his criticism and advice; and to Harlow Lindley of the Ohio State Archaeological and Historical Society, for his criticisms and for the use of materials in his possession. These three have read the manuscript, and for their comments and criticisms the author is again grateful. Henry J. Cadbury of Harvard and Elbert Russell and G. A. Nuermberger of Duke have made useful suggestions. For their reading of the manuscript and their criticisms, the writer thanks also Professors Charles S. Sydnor, Bayrd Still, and W. T. Laprade of Duke University.

R. K. N.

Durham, North Carolina
October 15, 1942

CONTENTS

CHAPTER	PAGE
I. The Argument	3
II. A Beginning at Organization	13
III. Free Produce Becomes a Quaker Movement	30
IV. The Search for Free Labor Products	60
V. George W. Taylor and His Work	83
VI. Propaganda and the Press	100
Appendix	117
Bibliography	120
Index	133

THE FREE PRODUCE MOVEMENT

CHAPTER I

The Argument

The slavery question was a disruptive force, not only between North and South, but also in many other units of society. It was responsible for a bitter sectionalism in those states of the Old Northwest touching the Ohio River. It made of the Methodist Episcopal Church two hostile camps which required almost a century to reconcile. The cleavage was only less marked among the Presbyterians and Baptists. The Quakers, on the other hand, had a long-standing record of opposition to slavery and were generally regarded as presenting a united front in the vanguard of the anti-slavery movement. This was not the case. The slavery question agitated, rent, and confused the Society of Friends, even as it did other denominations.

All Quakers condemned slavery; unfortunately they could not agree on the means and manner of opposing it. Then, much more than now, Quakers were a "peculiar people" who "mixed not in the world." Yet within their organization all shades of opinion existed, from the ultraconservative to the most radical. The great body of conservatives showed little interest in reforms and felt that Quakers had done their full duty by abolishing slavery among themselves. For them it was enough to repeat year after year their formal denunciation of slavery and to trust that the Lord in His own good time would destroy the evil. Beyond these conservatives stood a large body of liberals, flanked by a sizable number of radicals and a few fanatics.

Social reform was a primary interest with the radicals. They believed that it could be carried on side by side with their religious activity. The extreme radicals began by espousing abolition and proceeded from that to such other reforms as women's rights, temperance, peace, and the many fantastic schemes which were afloat in the nineteenth century. Those who were rather less radical riveted their attention on the abolition of slavery and did not sponsor other reforms until that was accomplished.

In the early nineteenth century many Friends belonged to the manumission societies and other mild organizations for the gradual abolition of slavery. When the abolition crusade aroused controversy, created emotional excitement, and took a political turn, the Society of Friends was forced to define its position. During the 1830's many liberal Friends joined abolition societies, while the conservatives held aloof. The latter, who generally controlled the Society, condemned Quaker membership in abolition societies as detrimental to religious unity. About 1840 they began to close their meetinghouses to abolition lecturers.

Liberal and radical Friends strongly objected to giving up their abolition activities, but in order to avoid trouble most of them withdrew from such "mixed" societies and formed their own anti-slavery societies with membership limited to Quakers. In many instances this concession was sufficient. In other sections the conservatives were still not satisfied. The result was that many individuals were disowned and there was a separation in the Society itself in Indiana. In seeking a satisfactory form of activity the liberals and radicals usually formed free produce societies, in which they agreed to boycott all products raised by slave labor, so far as that was possible.

Quakers' opposition to slavery had begun with condemnation of the slave trade. From this they advanced to a denunciation of slavery itself. Before the last Quaker had manumitted his last slave the most advanced members of the Society, among whom was John Woolman, propounded the argument that the use of goods produced by slave labor was as bad as slaveholding itself, for it gave to an owner the inducement to hold his slaves in bondage and provided economic support of the system. The receiver of stolen goods is as bad as the thief, they repeated again and again. Woolman joined the use of slave labor goods with the Quaker testimony against war by arguing that the seizure of slaves on the African coast was really an act of war. This made slaves prize goods, against the acceptance of which Quakers had testified for years.

It would be difficult to prove what person first felt it his duty to abstain from the use of slave labor products. That person may have been Ralph Sandiford (1693-1733), a native of Liverpool, who later migrated to Pennsylvania. His observation of slavery in the West Indies led him to the conclusion that it was wrong, an opinion which he continued to express during the remainder of his life. His views were further expounded in a tract entitled *The Mystery of Iniquity, in a Brief Examination of the Practice of the*

Times, published in 1729. Though threatened with legal action, Sandiford continued to defend his views of slavery. No specific evidence indicates that Sandiford abstained from the products of slave labor as such, although in his last years he lived very simply, being "conscientiously opposed to those habits of luxury which . . . had begun to be indulged in Pennsylvania."[1]

The first abstainer on record, however, was Benjamin Lay. Born at Colchester, England, in 1677, Lay went to Barbados in 1718 and there saw slavery at first hand. When he arrived at Philadelphia in 1731, he was already outspoken in his views on the subject. As he advanced in years, his eccentricity became notorious. He consistently refused to eat any food produced by slave labor, nor, in the houses of his friends, would he accept anything served by slaves. His clothing was made of tow which he spun himself, while his other peculiarities included vegetarianism, residence in a cavelike dwelling, and prolonged fasts.[2]

If Lay was perhaps the earliest abstainer from slave products, certainly John Woolman was the first to impress the idea upon his fellow Quakers. His journal for November 25, 1769, recorded his first statement on the subject. By trade a tailor, Woolman also pursued other activities, among which was frequently the making out of slave bills of sale. For many years he performed this service without giving much thought to the matter, but "After long and mournful exercise" he wished to explain "how things have opened in my mind":

. . . the oppression of the Slaves which I have seen . . . hath from time to time livingly revived on my mind, and under this exercise I

---

[1] Roberts Vaux, *Memoirs of the Lives of Benjamin Lay and Ralph Sandiford, Two of the Earliest Public Advocates for the Emancipation of the Enslaved Africans* (Philadelphia, 1815), pp. 59-73.

[2] *Ibid.*, pp. 13-30. While a merchant in Barbados, Lay freely expressed his opposition to slavery by befriending the slaves so that they assembled at his house on Sundays when he gave them food and religious instruction. His most startling action occurred during a yearly meeting session at Burlington, N. J., when he appeared in military cloak and sword, arose, and after making a few piercing denunciations of slaveholders, he slashed a concealed bladder containing pokeberry juice, to climax his remarks. Because of a spinal deformity Lay was only four feet and seven inches tall, which added to the peculiarity of his appearance. In spite of his eccentric behavior, Lay had many friends, among whom were Anthony Benezet and Benjamin Franklin. The latter published Lay's tract, *All Slave Keepers, That Keep the Innocent in Bondage, Apostates* . . . (1737). Lay died on Feb. 3, 1759, at the age of eighty-two (William Teignmouth Shore, *John Woolman; His Life and Our Times: Being a Study in Applied Christianity*, London, 1913, p. 61).

for some years past declined to gratify my pallate with those sugars. . . . I do not censure my Brethren in these things, but believe . . . the trading in or frequent use of any produce known to be raised by the labours of those who are under such lamentable oppression, hath appeared to be a subject which may yet more require the Serious consideration of the humble followers of Christ. . . . The number of those who decline the customary use of The West India produce . . . even amongst people truly pious . . . have not been very extensive.[3]

A third among the early abstainers was Warner Mifflin (1745-1798), the Delaware Friend, who about 1778 had his conscience roused on the subject by the running ashore of a prize vessel. During the remainder of the Revolutionary War he used no more imported goods, and in 1796 he expressed his convictions on the subject: "And being brought into deep feeling for the oppressions of the poor Africans in the West Indies, I have not been easy with indulging myself in using the produce of their labor since. . . ."[4]

The first woman known to express her views on the subject was Alice (Jackson) Lewis, the wife of Enoch Lewis, of Chester County, Pennsylvania. While she was attending Yearly Meeting at Philadelphia in the spring of 1806, she "laid this subject before that body, in a forcible and impressive address." This act was the culmination of her increasing scruples against the use of slave labor products. For some years previous to this she had "discriminated in her purchases for the family between the produce of free or slave labor; and as far as possible herself abstained from using any article of slave production."[5] At about the same time a London Friend, John Horn, felt such a strong conviction on the subject that, to

[3] John Woolman, *The Journal and Essays of John Woolman*, edited from the Original Manuscripts with a Biographical Introduction, by Amelia Mott Gummere (Philadelphia and London, 1922), p. 283.

[4] Warner Mifflin, *A Defense Against Aspersions, Cast Against Him on Account of His Endeavors to Promote Righteousness, Mercy and Peace among Mankind* (Philadelphia, 1796), pp. 19 f.; also printed in Hilda Justice (comp.), *Life and Ancestry of Warner Mifflin: Friend—Philanthropist—Patriot* (Philadelphia, 1905), p. 91.

[5] Joseph L. Lewis, *A Memoir of Enoch Lewis* (West Chester, Pa., 1882), p. 34. An examination of the MS Minutes of Philadelphia Yearly Meeting of Women Friends for the years 1804-10 shows no record of any such address by Alice Lewis. She was in 1806 a representative (i.e., delegate) from Concord Quarterly Meeting. This negative evidence from the Minutes cannot be taken as conclusive, since the minutes followed a set form and expression which varied little from year to year.

"ease" his mind, he urged all Quakers who might "feel their minds secretly burdened" by the use of West Indian sugar "not to stifle the smallest convictions of duty."[6]

Probably the strongest presentation of the subject in these early years came from the pen of Elias Hicks, who in 1811 first published his *Observations on the Slavery of the Africans and Their Descendants, and on the Use of the Produce of Their Labor*. This essay, in the form of nineteen queries and answers, covered most of the arguments ever advanced by advocates of the cause. Beginning with the assertion that slaves were prizes of war, he then deduced that the products of their labor were also prize goods. He proceeded to the question, "By what class of the people is the slavery of the Africans and their descendants supported and encouraged?" To this he replied, "Principally by the purchasers and consumers of the produce of the slaves' labour. . . ." This led him to ask what effect abstinence would have upon slaves and slaveholders. He argued that it would "meliorate . . . and abate" the "cruel bondage" of the former, and circumscribe the avarice of the latter. He concluded on a strong note of personal application by saying:

If we as individuals concerned in purchasing and consuming the produce of slavery, should imagine that our share in the transaction is so minute, that it cannot perceptibly increase the injury; let us recollect, that, though numbers partaking of a crime may diminish the shame, they cannot diminish its turpitude.[7]

[6] John Horn, *Some Considerations on the African Slave Trade, and the Use of West India Produce*, London, January 17, 1805 (G. Cooke, printer), a broadside. John Horn, the son of Joseph and Mary Horn, both Quakers, was born at Tring, Hertfordshire, England, in May, 1738. After learning the weaving trade he married, but within nine years his wife and three of his four children died. About 1781 he became a minister and thereafter performed many religious journeys until 1803, when his health became too feeble for such activity. Late in 1804 he wrote his *Considerations on the African Slave Trade*. . . . He died on March 13, 1805 (Lucy Edmunds, *A Short Sketch of the Life of Our Dear Friend John Horn; with Some of His Expressions towards His Close*. . . . Also, *Considerations on the African Slave Trade and the Use of West India Produce. First Published by Him in His Last Illness*, London, 1806, pp. 3-35).

[7] Elias Hicks, *Letters of Elias Hicks: Including also Observations on the Slavery of the Africans and Their Descendants, and on the Use of the Produce of Their Labor* (Philadelphia, 1861), pp. 8-20. This tract, first published in 1811, went through many later editions. Elias Hicks (1779-1830), a native of Long Island, N. Y., was a prominent minister in the Society of Friends. He is best known because of the doctrinal controversy which resulted in a separation throughout much of the Society (1827). Hicks's free produce

One of the most prominent Friends to practice abstinence was William Allen (1770-1843). At the age of eighteen he expressed his opposition to slavery. Some years later he concluded that

... one step farther may be taken by me, which is wanting to complete my testimony [against slavery] ... and which, if universally adopted would eventually put a stop to this enormous evil, and that is, disusing those commodities produced by the labour of slaves. And as sugar is, undoubtedly, one of the chief, I resolve, through divine assistance to persevere in the disuse of it until the slave trade shall be abolished.

To this resolution Allen adhered, even when the Russian emperor offered him tea with sugar produced by slave labor.[8]

Outside the Society of Friends one of the first persons to denounce the use of slave labor products was Thomas Branagan. Born in Dublin on December 28, 1774, of a prosperous family, he was brought up in (but later deserted) the Catholic faith and had the opportunity of ample educational advantages. He disliked school, however, and at the age of thirteen went to sea. During the succeeding years he saw much both of the slave trade and of privateering. About 1795 Branagan settled in Antigua, where he became an overseer on a sugar plantation. Here he remained for four years. This experience impressed upon him the barbarity of slavery as it then existed in the West Indies, and greatly influenced his later activities. About 1801 Branagan came to Philadelphia and in succeeding years devoted much of his time to anti-slavery writings. Among his earlier essays (written prior to 1807) was "Buying Stolen Goods Synonymous with Stealing," in which he asked:

... can a Christian ... buy and use the price and produce of human blood ... and who is it that does not know that the produce of the southern planters, as well as West India produce, is stolen

---

views increased the acrimony (Samuel Macpherson Janney, *An Examination of the Causes Which Led to the Separation of the Religious Society of Friends in America, in 1827-28*, Philadelphia, 1868, pp. 211-213).

[8] *Non-Slaveholder*, I, 108 (July, 1846); William Allen, *Life of William Allen, with Selections from His Correspondence* (3 vols., London, 1846-47), II, 265. William Allen (Aug. 29, 1770-Dec. 30, 1843), the son of a British Quaker silk manufacturer, early showed an aptitude for chemistry and in 1795 he opened a laboratory. He belonged to various scientific societies and also participated in numerous philanthropic enterprises, among which were abolition and education. In 1814 he was presented to visiting allied sovereigns as a typical Quaker. Here began his friendship with the Russian Emperor, Alexander I, whom Allen later visited.

with a vengeance, and that a vengeance must attend both the buyers and the sellers . . .?

He denounced the "fair devotees" of philanthropy who declaimed against slavery while at the same moment they sipped their tea "sweetened . . . by the sweat, the blood, the tears of their own tender sex. . . ." In a sterner tone he asserted:

Slavery depends on the consumption of the produce of its labour for support. Refuse this produce, and slavery MUST cease. Say not that individual influence is small. Every aggregate must be composed of a collection of individuals. . . . The number of those who have already refused the produce of slavery is large, it is increasing daily, and no bounds can be assigned to its future progress.[9]

The possibilities of individual abstinence when combined into a concerted effort were first demonstrated in 1791. The occasion was the unsuccessful effort to abolish the British slave trade. When the motion to effect that abolition failed in Parliament, a real popular protest arose throughout the British Isles. Led by Thomas Clarkson, who traveled some six thousand miles for the cause, as many as three hundred thousand persons, it was estimated, gave up the use of West India sugar in protest. The campaign was also characterized by numerous public meetings and a flood of petitions. Many pamphlets were also issued, among them, *A Short Sketch of the Evidence Delivered before a Committee of the House of Commons for the Abolition of the Slave Trade: To Which Is Added a Recommendation of the Subject to the Serious Attention of People in General*, by William Bell Crafton; *On the Propriety of Abstaining from West India Sugar and Rum*, by William Fox; and *Considerations Addressed to Professors of Christianity of Every Denomination, on the Impropriety of Consuming West-India Sugar and Rum, as Produced by the Oppressive Labour of Slaves*. The arguments in all this pamphlet propaganda were essentially the same. The authors reached the conclusion that if one family using five

[9] [Thomas Branagan,] *The Guardian Genius of the Federal Union; or, Patriotic Admonitions on the Signs of the Times, in Relation to the Evil Spirit of Party, Arising from the Root of All Our Evils, Human Slavery. Being Part of the Beauties of Philanthropy*, by a Philanthropist (2d ed., New York, 1840), pp. 13-19, 30-34. This volume contains twenty-three essays, of which the two here cited are "Memoirs of the Author" and "Buying Stolen Goods Synonymous with Stealing." Branagan died on June 13, 1843.

pounds of sugar a week would abstain for twenty-one months, it would prevent the enslavement and murder of one Negro. By other elaborate mathematical calculations they computed that 180,000 slaves had already been *consumed*. After detailing the horrors of the slave trade and West India slavery, they branded every consumer of West India produce as guilty of murder. A by-product of this movement was the advertisement by an enterprising chinaware merchant of sugar bowls "handsomely labelled in Gold Letters: 'East India Sugar not made by Slaves.' "[10] This British boycott of sugar was necessarily short-lived. It served, however, as an example of what could be done, and was very useful to later advocates of the cause.

At about the same time the post-Revolutionary opposition to slavery reached its climax in America. For a few years some abolitionists centered their enthusiastic attention upon the sugar maple as a potent agent in combating slavery. They confidently looked forward to the day when maple sugar would replace that of the West India cane in the markets of the world. Jacques Pierre Brissot de Warville, the French traveler, was among the most enthusiastic.

The Quakers [he said] have discerned in this production the means of destroying slavery. . . . Whenever . . . the production of this divine tree . . . may fill the markets of Europe . . . [it] will ruin the sale of that of the islands—a produce washed with the tears and the blood of slaves. . . .[11]

Gilbert Imlay, another early traveler, expressed the same faith in maple sugar without, however, applying it so emphatically to the slavery question.[12] Dr. Benjamin Rush was one of the most prominent men to give attention to the idea at this time. He also looked

[10] *Considerations on the Slave Trade and the Consumption of West Indian Produce* (London, 1791), pp. 1, 14; Thomas Clarkson, *The History of the Rise, Progress, and Accomplishment of the Abolition of the African Slave-Trade by the British Parliament* (2 vols., London, 1808), II, 346-354. Bibliographers are not agreed on the authorship of the pamphlets mentioned above. B. Henderson, *East India Sugar Basins* (n.p., n.d.), a broadside.

[11] Jacques Pierre Brissot de Warville, *New Travels in the United States of America. Performed in* 1788: *Translated from the French* (London, 1792), pp. 301-306.

[12] Gilbert Imlay, *A Description of the Western Territory of North America: Containing a Succinct Account of Its Soil, Climate, Natural History, Population, Agriculture, Manners and Customs, in a Series of Letters to a Friend in England* (Dublin, 1793), reprinted in Great American Historical Classics Series (Bowling Green, Ohio, 1919), pp. 113-118, 184.

upon it as a solution to the slavery question. It was claimed that Thomas Jefferson went so far as to plant a large grove of maple trees. In any case he wrote in 1790:

Late difficulties in the sugar trade have excited attention to our sugar trees, and it seems fully believed by judicious persons, that we cannot only supply our own demand, but make for exportation. . . . What a blessing to substitute a sugar which requires only the labor of children for that which is said to render the slavery of blacks necessary.[13]

The propriety of using products of slave labor was first to come before an organized body in this country in 1796. The occasion was the third American Convention for Promoting the Abolition of Slavery and Improving the Condition of the African Race, held in Philadelphia. The committee "to report to the Convention the objects proper for its attention" included in its recommendations

That, as one mean[s] of promoting its interests, they [i.e., the abolition societies represented in the Convention] be earnestly solicited to display a marked preference of all such commodities as are of the culture or manufacture of freemen, to those which are cultivated or manufactured by slaves.

This was seconded in the report of the committee to prepare the address "to the different Abolition Societies," which urged "a marked preference" for free labor articles, and added, "In this way every individual may discountenance oppression. . . ."[14] Which member or members of these committees were responsible for the introduction of a statement urging abstinence from slave labor products is an unsolved question. The most likely supposition, however, is that it was a member of either the Pennsylvania or Delaware

[13] Jefferson to Benjamin Vaughan, June 27, 1790, Thomas Jefferson, *The Writings of Thomas Jefferson* . . . (20 vols., Washington, 1904), VIII, 50; Mary Stoughton Locke, *Anti-Slavery in America, from the Introduction of African Slaves to the Prohibition of the Slave Trade (1619-1808)*, Radcliffe College Monographs, No. 11 (Boston, 1901), pp. 189 f.

[14] American Convention for Promoting the Abolition of Slavery and Improving the Condition of the African Race, *Minutes of the Proceedings of the Third Convention of Delegates from the Abolition Societies Established in Different Parts of the United States, Assembled at Philadelphia* . . . (Philadelphia, 1796), pp. 16, 28. The Committee on the Objects Proper for the Attention of the Society consisted of: Joseph Bloomfield (N. J.), Elihu Hubbard Smith (N. Y.), William Rogers (Pa.), William Poole (Del.), Joseph Townsend (Md.), Samuel Miller (N. Y.), and Micajah Davis (Va.). The Committee to Prepare the Address had as members: Caspar Wistar, Samuel Powell Griffitts, and Samuel Miller.

society. Warner Mifflin had been one of the delegates from Delaware at the first convention held in 1794. Twenty years passed before the subject again came to the attention of the American Convention, but a beginning was made in 1816 when that body attributed the evils of slavery to "the love of money" and added that the "increasing demand for the produce of the southern states had induced the planter to offer high prices for slaves." In 1823 the Convention subscribed for two hundred copies of *A Letter to M. Jean-Baptiste Say, on the Comparative Expense of Free and Slave Labour*, by Adam Hodgson, which was being republished by the New York Manumission Society.[15] The meeting of 1825 resolved to offer a prize for the best exemplification of that idea in actual terms of profit realized from each sort of labor. Isaac Barton and Thomas Earle of the Pennsylvania delegation offered resolutions recommending that abolitionists give up the use of slave labor products and that premiums should be offered for sugar, cotton, rice, and tobacco which had indubitably been raised by free labor. The Convention showed little enthusiasm, however, and referred the resolution to the next session.[16] To that assemblage, convened in 1826, Isaac Barton presented identical resolutions, which, this time, were adopted and incorporated into the Address to the Abolition, Manumission, and Anti-Slavery Societies throughout the United States. Endorsement also came from the Delaware Society for Promoting the Abolition of Slavery and from the Anti-Slavery Society of Maryland, where Benjamin Lundy had pushed the subject at a state convention. Lundy's boundless energy in the anti-slavery cause was to provide a strong new force in the coming years.[17]

[15] American Convention . . . , *Minutes* (1816), p. 4; (1823), p. 24. Hodgson's letter to Say is an elaborate discussion setting forth, on purely economic grounds, the real economy of free labor. It did not advocate free labor as a moral or religious duty.

[16] American Convention . . . , *Minutes* (1825), pp. 17, 22.

[17] *Genius of Universal Emancipation*, IV, 164 f. (Aug., 1825); V, 389 (Aug. 5, 1826); VI, 73 ff., 81 (Nov. 25, Dec. 2, 1826). Lundy organized the Anti-Slavery Society of Maryland on Aug. 25, 1825. Its first annual convention adopted these statements: "We fear one of the most prominent causes of its [slavery's] continuance among us, is owing too much to the encouragement held out to slave holders by purchasing their produce; for according to the demand so is the inducement. . . . Therefore, *Resolved*, That the time has arrived when the friends of emancipation should, so far as is practicable, take a bold and vigorous stand against the use of all articles, the produce of slave labor. . . ." This resolution was to be forwarded to the American Convention.

CHAPTER II

A BEGINNING AT ORGANIZATION

It was inevitable that some kind of organization should be formed to advance the idea of boycotting slave labor goods. The first was apparently a "little society" founded at Wilmington, Delaware, in June, 1826, to work for the extinction of slavery in that state, and to consider the propriety of "consuming the products of *slave-labor*."[1] Organization was not perfected until December 21, 1826, when the Wilmington Society for the Encouragement of Free Labor adopted its constitution and elected officers. The constitution proclaimed that "Its object shall be to encourage the cultivation of such articles by Freemen as are now produced by the labor of slaves; and to collect and disseminate information calculated to promote the object of this Association." An acting committee of six members was to seek means of obtaining free labor goods, and was to encourage any measures which might promote "Free labor in the slave districts of the United States. . . ." Meetings of the society were to be held quarterly, and anyone might become a member by signing the constitution and paying fifty cents.[2]

In 1827 the Society was represented at the meeting of the American Convention for Promoting the Abolition of Slavery and Improving the Condition of the African Race. To this assemblage the Wilmington society presented an address detailing their purposes. The work of their acting committee was summarized in their statement that considerable cotton could be had, "produced in the slave districts of the United States, untouched by slaves, some of which has been manufactured in this vicinity, and is now for sale, at fair prices." But when it came to groceries the story was less

[1] *Genius of Universal Emancipation*, V, 348 (July 1, 1826).
[2] *Ibid.*, VI, 129 (Jan. 27, 1827). [The numbering of this journal is very irregular, there having been several series, each with separately numbered volumes. To avoid confusion a straight numbering of volumes, beginning with I and running through XIV, has been adopted. From 1825 to 1828 the paper was issued weekly; the remainder was a monthly periodical. On numerous occasions it was not issued at all.]

Officers elected at this first meeting were: President, Lea Pusey; Vice-President, John Reynolds; Secretary, William P. Richards; Treasurer, Charles Canby; Acting Committee, Isaac Peirce, Dr. William Gibbons, Joseph G. Rowland, Eli Hilles, Benjamin Webb, and E. W. Gilbert.

encouraging, for "it is found that they can not yet be procured in sufficient quantities, at prices to compete with like articles produced by slave labor, coffee alone excepted."[3] After this vigorous beginning the Wilmington society dropped from the picture, although it was in existence at the beginning of 1829.

The Free Produce Society of Pennsylvania was only a few months later in origin than its Wilmington counterpart, and was destined to a considerably longer existence. The preliminary meeting occurred on September 9, 1826, and was described by the philanthropist, James Mott, in a letter to his parents.

I have this evening attended a meeting of about forty Friends to take into consideration the propriety of forming an association to procure cotton, sugar, etc. raised by free labour. A committee of twelve was appointed to consider what means will best promote the object, and report to an adjourned meeting to be held the last of next week. This concern has spread very much in this city and neighbourhood within a few years, and I believe will eventually prevail.[4]

Actual organization was not achieved until January 8, 1827. The constitution declared that the use of slave labor products supported slavery, that abolition would be promoted by the substitution of free labor products, and that the economy of free labor should be proved to slaveholders.

Sixty-four men signed the constitution as members. Most of them were Quakers, and several continued to be active in the anti-slavery movement for many years. The first officers elected were: William Rawle, President; Thomas McClintock, Secretary; Benjamin Tucker, Vice-President; Henry M. Zollickoffer, Treasurer; and the Corresponding Committee composed of Abraham L. Pennock, Isaac Barton, Thomas Shipley, James Mott, George Peterson, Samuel Smith, Edwin P. Atlee, Nathan Shoemaker, Jonathan Palmer, Jr., and John Bouvier. Other prominent members included Isaac Tatem Hopper, William S. Hallowell, Joseph Parrish, and Joseph Parker.[5]

[3] American Convention . . . , *Minutes* (1827), p. 46.
[4] Ann Davis Hallowell, *James and Lucretia Mott: Life and Letters*, Edited by Their Granddaughter (Boston, 1884), p. 96.
[5] William Rawle (1759-1836), a prominent lawyer, was very active in civic affairs. Abraham L. Pennock (1786-1868) was at different times an officer in various anti-slavery societies, and was a delegate to the American Convention for the first time in 1817. He was later editor of the *Non-*

This Corresponding Committee was directed to communicate with anyone, anywhere "favorable to the labor of Freemen; and to the consumption of their products" in order to open the market for such goods. The Committee was also to circulate such information as it collected, and to emphasize the logic of the free labor cause. In January, 1827, the Society was given the use of a room in Clarkson Hall "free of expense" for its quarterly meetings.[6]

Pursuant to instructions, the Corresponding Committee, on April 11, 1827, issued a circular, probably in broadside form, expressing a desire to assist nonslaveholders in slave areas to find better markets for their crops, so as to prove thereby the superiority of free labor. Then followed a questionnaire asking for information, with names and addresses of individual farmers who were producing cotton, rice, sugar, molasses, tobacco, etc., by free labor. Other questions inquired how many persons might be induced to raise any of these products by free labor if assured of a market; how many consumers would purchase them "at a small advance above the market price"; and how many would buy them if sold at the same price as slave labor goods.[7]

When the American Convention assembled in 1827, the Free

Slaveholder and a member of the Board of Managers of the Philadelphia Free Produce Association. Thomas McClintock was the author of one or more anti-slavery tracts. Benjamin Tucker died on June 24, 1833. Isaac Barton (1795-1868) had been active in the American Convention. Thomas Shipley (1787-1836) was also president of the Pennsylvania Society for Promoting the Abolition of Slavery, etc. James Mott (1788-1868) is best known for his philanthropic and anti-slavery activities. It was about this time that he gave up his cotton-trade business because he felt it to be wrong. Edwin P. Atlee, a Philadelphia physician, was very active in the anti-slavery movement. John Bouvier (1787-1851) was born in France. After coming to the United States he was a newspaper editor and later became a lawyer. Joseph Parrish (1779-1840) was a physician. Isaac T. Hopper (1771-1852) was most prominent as a Friend (Hicksite) who was disowned chiefly because of his views on slavery.

[6] Free Produce Society of Pennsylvania, *Constitution* . . . (Philadelphia [, 1827]), pp. 1-12. This constitution was also printed in full in the *Genius of Universal Emancipation*, VII, 2 f. (July 4, 1827); Pennsylvania Society for Promoting the Abolition of Slavery, for the Relief of Free Negroes Unlawfully Held in Bondage, and for Improving the Condition of the African Race, Minutes (MS), Jan. 18, 1827, III (1825-47), 57.

Clarkson Hall stood at Sixth and Cherry streets. Presumably it was owned by the Pennsylvania Society for Promoting the Abolition of Slavery, etc., who conducted in it a school for Negro children and adults. It was used for many years as an auditorium for anti-slavery meetings.

[7] *Genius of Universal Emancipation*, VII, 11 (July 14, 1827).

Produce Society of Pennsylvania was represented alongside the "Delaware Free Labor Society of Wilmington." Benjamin Lundy, a delegate from Maryland, was the prime mover in placing the subject before the Convention. After getting a committee appointed to consider "the subject of free and slave labor and the propriety of further encouraging the use of productions not contaminated by slavery," Lundy introduced a resolution to appoint a committee to investigate the sources of free labor goods and report to the next meeting what experiments had been made in the use of free labor with a view to showing its advantages over slave labor.[8]

The Address of the Free Produce Society of Pennsylvania to the American Convention dwelt on the superiority of free labor, the need for proof thereof by actual demonstration, and the necessity of creating a demand for free produce. It presented abstinence as a proper, just, and reasonable means of opposing slavery. The position of these two societies was endorsed by the Pennsylvania Society for Promoting the Abolition of Slavery, which had determined early in 1827 to bring the subject before the Convention.[9]

At the meeting of the American Convention in December, 1829, the Free Produce Society of Pennsylvania was again represented and again offered an address reviewing its activities. They asserted that "It is no more than the exercise of an elective franchise, for the free man to purchase the products of the labour of freemen, in preference to that of Slaves." To prove the vitality of the cause in Pennsylvania, delegates announced the formation of the Female Association for Promoting the Manufacture and Use of Free Cotton.[10]

The first preliminary meeting of this society, with thirteen women present, was held in January, 1829. Within a few months membership mounted to more than a hundred, organization was completed, and a constitution adopted. With the sum realized from dues the Society first bought a little muslin, and then bought several

[8] American Convention . . . , *Minutes* (1827), pp. 3-10. Members of the committee were: Benjamin Lundy, Thomas Shipley, Joseph Parker, William Kesley, and David Scholfield. Their report, given in 1828, listed various areas where free labor products could be obtained.

[9] American Convention . . . , *Minutes* (1827), pp. 41 f.; Pennsylvania Society for Promoting the Abolition of Slavery, etc., Minutes (MS), Jan. 4, 1827, III (1825-47), 66. Each society represented in the American Convention prepared an address which was read before the Convention. Delegates from the Pennsylvania Free Produce Society were Joseph Parrish, Joseph Parker, and Jesse W. Newport.

[10] American Convention . . . , *Minutes* (1829), pp. 57-60.

bales of cotton which were manufactured into apron checks and bedticking.[11] The Society appealed to women generally to exert their influence by abstinence from slave labor products, and by instilling in their "offspring a deep-felt sense of their duty [to give] the preference to the products of free labor."

Let societies be formed among you to promote this.... It is true, some inconveniences will at first be unavoidable, the texture of your garments will perhaps be coarser than that of your accustomed wear, but they will cling less heavily around your forms, for the sighs of the broken-hearted will not linger among their folds.[12]

In October, 1829, the Society reported that slightly more than 2,500 pounds of free upland cotton had been "manufactured into ginghams, checks, bedtickings, stripes, knitting and sewing cotton, and cotton hose."[13] The cotton here referred to was obtained from Nathan Hunt, Jr., of Guilford County, North Carolina, who collected it from Quaker and other nonslaveholding farmers in that area.[14] In June, 1830, the committee reported no profit, but also no loss on its transactions, and hence felt encouraged. They then had some 2,500 yards of goods available. Men of the Pennsylvania Free Produce Society had voluntarily raised $1,000 as a loan without interest for one year so that the women might expand their operations.[15]

At the end of a year the demand for free labor cotton goods had outrun the Society's ability to supply them. At this juncture, however, Nathan Hunt, Jr., was ready to send forty bales of free labor cotton. Since this amount was far beyond the finances of the Society, they considered it "expedient to engage a person of veracity to purchase it on his own responsibility, keep it separate from other cotton, and have it manufactured into such goods as are best suited to the market. One of this character has presented himself...." A month later thirty bales of the cotton had been received and were in process of manufacture.[16] This made a stock of several thousand yards of cloth of various kinds which apparently was sold without trouble.

The Society continued very vigorous throughout its second

[11] *Genius of Universal Emancipation*, X, 4 (Sept. 2, 1829).
[12] *Ibid.*, X, 12 (Sept. 16, 1829).   [13] *Ibid.*, X, 58 (Oct. 30, 1829).
[14] *Ibid.*, X, 68 (Nov. 6, 1829).   [15] *Ibid.*, XI, 43 f. (June, 1830).
[16] *Ibid.*, XI, 10, 25 (April, May, 1830). The person was probably Samuel Comly, mentioned in the report.

year, with monthly reports of activities and manufacturing. In April, 1831, they noted the receipt of some free labor cotton from Santo Domingo and two bales from South Carolina. The Society existed in the spring of 1833, but apparently the first enthusiasm had waned, and, doubtless, difficulties had been encountered. The organization probably faded out of existence shortly thereafter, or perhaps the ramifications of business appeared to be going beyond the proper sphere of feminine activities.[17]

In any event it was the Free Produce Society of Pennsylvania which carried on the burden of the work. The members were optimistic in 1829 over the prospect of obtaining free labor products. In addition to the cotton sent by Nathan Hunt, Jr., they were assured that nonslaveholding farmers near Washington, North Carolina, would soon be raising cotton, while in the same area many of them raised a little rice. The Society hoped that its purchases would lead to the growing of more rice. The search for sugar was the most difficult. From Puerto Rico they first obtained twelve hogsheads of sugar raised by a Creole planter who was personally opposed to slavery. They expected to obtain one hundred hogsheads of sugar annually from this source, and supplement it with maple sugar and maple syrup. During 1829 the Society purchased over $4,000 worth of free labor sugar and molasses. Procurement and sale of free grocery products were carried on by Charles Pierce in Philadelphia. In 1831 his sales exceeded $5,000, while by that time several other small stores had been set up.[18]

There is no doubt that the Free Produce Society of Pennsylvania continued to exist, but its status is another matter. In 1837 it addressed the special and final meeting of the American Convention, wherein it lamented the apathy of its members, but reaffirmed its faith in the cause and noted the increased abstinence and readier means for obtaining free labor goods.[19]

Meantime there were a few other small societies. Two of them, which were directly the work of the Free Produce Society of Pennsylvania, were the Colored Free Produce Society of Pennsyl-

---

[17] *Genius of Universal Emancipation*, XI, 199 (April, 1831); XII, 11, 162 (May, 1831, March, 1832); XIII, 110 (May, 1833).

[18] *Ibid.*, X, 58 (Oct. 30, 1829); XI, 194 (April, 1831). Rice could be obtained from the East Indies, but the quality was described as poor and the price very high.

[19] American Convention . . . , *Minutes* (1837), pp. 20 f.

vania and the Colored Female Free Produce Society. Both were organized at the beginning of 1831. Benjamin Lundy addressed the men's society on April 18, 1831, and induced them to appropriate ten dollars to be added to a premium offered for free labor rice. The Female Society was organized and carried on in conjunction with the "Female Free Cotton Society."[20]

The free produce movement west of the Alleghanies had its first advocates in eastern Ohio. In 1826 the Aiding Abolition Society of Monroe County, Ohio, issued an "Address to the Merchants of the State of Ohio and Elsewhere" which declared that merchants as well as their customers were the supporters of slavery. It called on the people of Ohio to co-operate in using as little slave labor goods as possible and expressed the hope that every merchant would support the cause.[21] On October 26, 1833, the Free Produce and Anti-Slavery Society of Monroe County, Ohio, was formed "to abolish slavery in the United States, and particularly to abstain, as far as practicable, from the produce of slave-labor. . . ." Salem, in Columbiana County, Ohio, was, however, the great anti-slavery center in that state. On January 6, 1827, the Salem Abolition and Colonization Society was formed.[22] Its later history is obscure, but the breath of revival reached it on January 19, 1834, when the New Garden Anti-Slavery Society, an auxiliary of the American Anti-Slavery Society, was formed. The New Garden society embodied in its constitution the determination of "abstaining, as far as practicable, from the use of the PRODUCTS OF SLAVERY. . . ." The Convention which organized the Ohio Anti-Slavery Society in 1835 declared that it would "practically testify against slavery, by giving a uniform preference to the products of free labor."[23]

In September, 1832, the Free Produce Association of Green Plain (Clark County, Ohio) was organized. Apparently it began as early as 1829 in a very small way among a few Quaker women "to whom the sweets of the cane, cultivated amid sighs and tears, have become loathsome; to whom gorgeous apparel, purchased at

[20] *Genius of Universal Emancipation*, XI, 194 (Supplement, April, 1831); XII, 12, 57 (May, Aug., 1831).
[21] *Ibid.*, V, 338 (June 24, 1826); *Liberator*, IV, 170 (Oct. 25, 1834).
[22] *Genius of Universal Emancipation*, VI, 183 (April 14, 1827); *Liberator*, IV, 45 (March 22, 1834).
[23] Ohio Anti-Slavery Society, *Proceedings of the Ohio Anti-Slavery Convention: Held at Putnam, on the Twenty-second, Twenty-third, and Twenty-fourth of April, 1835* (n.p., n.d.), p. 9.

the price of blood, hath become a burden too heavy to be borne."[24] They wrote of their efforts to the "Ladies' Free Produce Society of Philadelphia" and sought to buy free labor goods from the latter. The Green Plain society's first annual report a year later at least showed it to be in a flourishing condition and still earnest in the cause. Its activities, if any, are not indicated in the report. In near-by Harrison County (Ohio) the Harrisville Free Produce and Anti-Slavery Society was likewise inquiring about the purchase of free labor dry goods from Philadelphia.[25]

During these years other small societies which at least endorsed the free produce principle were organized in Pennsylvania. One of these, the Centreville Abolition Society of Washington County, had among its leaders Jesse Kenworthy, who in 1825 and 1826 was urging abstinence on its members. As early as 1826 individual inquiries about free labor cotton came from Chester County, Pennsylvania, where, in 1833, the Oxford Free Produce Society was formed. On November 2, 1838, this group dissolved and reorganized as the Union Free Produce Society, an auxiliary of the American Free Produce Association which it had helped to form earlier that year. The Union Free Produce Society was active for at least seven years. It immediately made plans to open a free produce store. The meetings of 1839 and 1840 were much occupied with discussions of the proposition that the use of slave labor produce is "essentially sinful under all circumstances." They investigated the existence of slavery in British India, and continued their annual meetings through 1845, after which this society disappeared.[26] A third, the Clarkson Anti-Slavery Association of Citizens of Lancaster and Chester Counties, Pennsylvania, was organized late in 1832. By 1834 its members were asking, "Is it consistent with the principles of Abolitionists, to use the products of slave labor?"[27]

The feeble and scattered efforts of the free produce cause were

[24] *Genius of Universal Emancipation*, X, 68 (Nov. 6, 1829); XIII, 77 (March, 1833).

[25] *Ibid.*, XIII, 77 (March, 1833); XIV, 13 (Jan., 1834).

[26] *Ibid.*, IV, 11 (Supplement, 1825); 187 f. (Feb. 11, 1826); *Pennsylvania Freeman* (Philadelphia), Feb. 21, May 9, 1839, Sept. 10, 1840, July 28, Nov. 3, 1841, Jan. 2, May 22, 1845; *Free Labor Advocate and Anti-Slavery Chronicle* (Newport, Wayne Co., Ind.), I, 294 f. (Nov. 9, 1841).

The first president of the Union Free Produce Association was William Brosius (1798-1887), a member and minister of Penn's Grove Monthly Meeting, and very active in many phases of the anti-slavery cause.

[27] *Liberator*, IV, 145 (Sept. 13, 1834).

soon to feel the stimulation of that sudden growth of abolition activity which began in 1831. The free produce principle distinctly belonged to the Quakers, was associated with the older abolitionism, and was publicized chiefly by Benjamin Lundy through the *Genius of Universal Emancipation*. It was now to be adopted by many who became leading abolitionists. Among these was William Lloyd Garrison, whose advocacy of the boycott idea was unquestionably due to his association with Lundy. So strong was this influence that Garrison in his "Declaration of Sentiments" proclaimed, "We shall encourage the labor of freemen rather than that of slaves, by giving a preference to their productions," when he organized the American Anti-Slavery Society in 1833.[28] Garrison continued to be an earnest advocate of the free labor principle for the next five or six years—in fact, until the complexities and ramifications of the abolition movement turned his attention to other things. Theodore Weld's statement during the same period shows the attitude of many abolitionists:

In lecturing [he said] it has been my great endeavor to push the main point. . . . I have dwelt little upon *collateral* principles—such as abstinence from the products of slave labor—not because it is not a duty, for so I believe, and so have practiced for years—but because *mind* acts, upon a collateral principle, *spontaneously*, if it be *first* anchored upon the main principle.[29]

Likewise, many of the local anti-slavery societies organized between 1833 and 1836 adopted the boycott as a collateral principle. This was almost certain to be the case wherever a sufficient number of Quakers participated to wield an influence. The idea was popular with women's societies and was considered a peculiarly appropriate tenet for them since it so closely concerned household economy.[30]

---

[28] American Anti-Slavery Society, *The Declaration of Sentiments and Constitution of the American Anti-Slavery Society* . . . (New York, 1837), p. 6; *Liberator*, IV, 101 (June 28, 1834). A committee recommended offering premiums for free labor goods in 1834.

[29] Theodore D. Weld to J. F. Robinson, May 1, 1836; Angelina Grimké Weld to Elizabeth Pease, Aug. 14, 1839 (Theodore Dwight Weld, Angelina Grimké Weld, and Sarah Grimké, *Letters . . . 1822-1844*, ed. Gilbert H. Barnes and Dwight L. Dumond, 2 vols., New York, 1934, I, 296; II, 782); *Non-Slaveholder*, II, 185 (April, 1847). Before 1847 Garrison turned completely away from the free labor idea and considered it a waste of time, when there were so many more practical things to be done.

[30] *Liberator*, II, 110 (July 14, 1832); IV, 61 (April 19, 1834); Boston Female Anti-Slavery Society, *Report* (2d ed., Boston, 1836), p. 79; Rhode

It was a subject of deliberation in the Anti-Slavery Convention of American Women. First assembled at New York in 1837, this group listened to a letter from the Free Produce Society of Oxford, Pennsylvania, after which Lucretia Mott offered a resolution, requiring a "prayerful examination" of women's duty in the matter of using slave labor products. The Convention issued *An Appeal to the Women of the Nominally Free States*, which devoted four pages to decrying the use of slave labor products. Herein they argued that free labor goods would be provided as soon as there was a demand; meanwhile women should gladly "suffer the inconvenience of deprivation, and then will *you*, dear sisters, become the favored instruments in the Lord's hand. . . ."[31] The next year Thankful Southwick of Boston offered a resolution "That it is the duty of all . . . to make the *most vigorous efforts* to procure for the use of their families the products of *free labor* . . . ," while Abby Kelley's resolution avowed "That we are very deeply implicated in the sin of using our brother's service without wages. . . ."[32]

Meanwhile, men in the Society of Friends (particularly the Hicksite branch) were stirring in the cause. Charles Marriott had begun to advocate the free labor principle as early as 1824. Eleven of his essays published at various times were in 1835 issued together as *An Address to the Members of the Religious Society of Friends, on the Duty of Declining the Use of the Products of Slave Labour*. Therein he reviewed all the arguments on the subject, he dwelt on Quaker testimony against prize goods and war, he appealed to the women, and he avowed that nothing but Quaker unfaithfulness in maintaining a consistent testimony against slavery had thus long

---

Island State Anti-Slavery Society, *Proceedings of the Rhode-Island Anti-Slavery Convention, Held in Providence, on the 2d, 3d and 4th of February, 1836* (Providence, 1836), p. 59.

[31] Two conventions were held, one in 1837 and the other in 1838. Anti-Slavery Convention of American Women. 1st, New York, 1837. *Proceedings* . . . (New York, 1837), pp. 12, 13; *An Appeal to the Women of the Nominally Free States* . . . (New York, 1837), pp. 24-28; *National Enquirer and Constitutional Advocate of Universal Liberty*, July 1, 8, 1837.

[32] Anti-Slavery Convention of American Women. 2d, Philadelphia, 1838. *Proceedings of a Convention Held in Philadelphia, May 15-18, 1838* (Philadelphia, 1838), pp. 7 f.; *Address to Anti-Slavery Societies* (Philadelphia, 1838), pp. 10 f. Abigail (Kelley) Foster (1810-1887) was born in Pelham, Mass. She abandoned teaching in 1837 to lecture in the abolition cause, and after 1850 she became a leader in the women's rights movement. In 1845 she married Stephen Symonds Foster, with whom she had been associated in abolition lecture tours.

prevented incorporation into the Discipline of an article requiring the boycott of slave labor products.[33]

This and other influences worked together during the next three years to carry the cause to new heights of achievement. Among the many bodies which assembled at Pennsylvania Hall[34] in May, 1838, was the Requited Labor Convention, which initiated the second effort towards an organized boycott of slave labor goods. It is impossible to determine just what forces were behind this new action. During the preceding months local anti-slavery societies had sprung up with bewildering rapidity in the Philadelphia area. They represented all shades of opinion from the most radical to the relatively staid. William C. Betts, one of the leaders in the effort, was a member of the Philadelphia City Anti-Slavery Society and the City and County Anti-Slavery Society.[35] The first call was sent out by the Clarkson Anti-Slavery Society of Chester County, Pennsylvania. Its members were as radical as could be found among Quakers anywhere, and later formed the nucleus which became Pennsylvania Yearly Meeting of Progressive Friends.[36] Among

[33] Pp. 12, 17. Charles Marriott (1782-1843) was born in Lancashire, England, the son of Henry and Margaret Marriott. About 1800 the family moved to Hudson, N. Y. Charles Marriott, prominent in a religious capacity as well as active in the anti-slavery cause, wrote for the *Genius of Universal Emancipation* and the *Liberator*. His greatest interest was to bring the Society of Friends to a firmer stand against slavery. To this end he wrote the above-mentioned tract, which the Meeting for Sufferings refused to endorse. When his friends joined him in publishing it on his own responsibility, Marriott, Isaac T. Hopper, and James S. Gibbons were disowned. Marriott then joined the American Anti-Slavery Society and became active in publishing the *Anti-Slavery Standard* (New York Association of Friends for the Relief of Those Held in Slavery, &c., *Testimony Concerning Charles Marriott, Deceased*, New York, 1844, pp. 1-15).

[34] Pennsylvania Hall was erected with funds raised by voluntary subscription, under the direction of a board of citizens known as the Pennsylvania Hall Association. The building was dedicated on May 15, 1838, as a "temple of free speech" and burned by a mob two days thereafter, in protest against the anti-slavery meetings being held there.

[35] William C. Betts (Jan. 22, 1813-June 27, 1844) was also a charter member of the Association of Friends for Advocating the Cause of the Slave, etc. He presided at the Requited Labor Convention, and was in 1839 and 1840 secretary of the American Free Produce Association and a member of its committee on manufactures. For a time his house was the depository for the goods manufactured. Betts's untimely death from lockjaw at the age of thirty-one deprived the anti-slavery movement of an energetic leader.

[36] Progressive or Congregational Friends were formed chiefly of Hicksite radicals who were dissatisfied with the Quaker stand on slavery and other social questions. The movement centered at Kennett Square, Pa., where

the societies invited to participate was the Pennsylvania Society for Promoting the Abolition of Slavery, &c., whose president stiffly declined "engaging in the proposed Convention." The general call was addressed to "Anti-Slavery Societies and Individuals throughout the United States." Some 271 delegates representing 23 anti-slavery societies (chiefly in Pennsylvania and New Jersey) were in attendance.[37] They immediately proceeded to form a "National Requited Labor Association" by appointing committees to draft a constitution, to determine the agenda, to "prepare and publish an Address on the duty of abstaining from the produce of slave labor . . . ," and to seek sources of free labor produce.

After two days of discussion the convention was forced to suspend its deliberations on account of the burning of Pennsylvania Hall on the night of May 17-18 and the mob spirit which prevailed in Philadelphia for several days. On September 5, 1838, the Requited Labor Convention reassembled (with fifty-seven delegates present), adopted the constitution which established the American Free Produce Association, and elected officers. Other business included proposals to establish free produce stores, to induce some manufacturers to use free labor cotton exclusively, and to raise money for the maintenance of an agent. After long discussion the fundamental resolution was adopted: "That as slaves are robbed of fruits of their toil, all who partake of those fruits are participants in the robbery and . . . we earnestly recommend to all abolitionists to en-

---

the Yearly Meeting of Progressive Friends assembled annually from 1853 to 1941. Green Plain Quarterly Meeting (Ohio) joined the movement in 1848, after being "laid down" for insubordination by Indiana Yearly Meeting. A similar break took place among Friends around Collins Center, N. Y. The slavery question was largely responsible for the original break, but in later years Progressive Friends sponsored many unpopular social reforms.

[37] *Pennsylvania Freeman*, March 15, 1838, June 19, 1845; Pennsylvania Hall Association, *History of Pennsylvania Hall*, pp. 127-135; Pennsylvania Society for Promoting the Abolition of Slavery, etc., Minutes (MS), April 26, 1838, III (1825-47), 330.

The societies participating in the Convention were: Clarkson Anti-Slavery Society, City and County A.S.S., Lynn (Mass.) A.S.S., Kennett A.S.S., Wilberforce A.S.S., Junior A.S.S., Association of Friends for Advocating the Cause of the Slave, etc., Oxford (Pa.) Free Produce Association, Northern Liberties A.S.S., Colerain A.S.S., Burlington City A.S.S., Buckingham Female A.S.S., Delaware County A.S.S., Lynn Female A.S.S., Kimberton A.S.S., Snowhill and Mount Zion A.S.S., Philadelphia City A.S.S., Frankford A.S.S., Spring Garden A.S.S., Bucks County A.S.S., West Chester A.S.S., East Fallowfield A.S.S., and Philadelphia Female A.S.S.

courage the furnishing of the market with free goods, by purchasing and using such only as are of this class."

The list of officers is most interesting. The president was Gerrit Smith. Vice-presidents were William Bassett, Abraham L. Pennock, William H. Johnson, all Friends, and Lewis Tappan, the philanthropist. The secretaries were Daniel L. Miller, Jr., and Lewis C. Gunn, and the treasurer Lucretia Mott, all Friends. The executive committee consisted of Charles C. Burleigh (the abolitionist and editor), Henry Grew, William C. Betts, John H. Cavender, Caleb Clothier (a Philadelphia Friend), Lydia White (who long operated a free produce store in Philadelphia), David Ellis, Sidney Ann Lewis, Martha Hampton, Sarah Pugh, and Alice Eliza Hambleton, all members of the Society of Friends. This list of officers exemplifies the cosmopolitan character of the movement at this initial stage. All varieties of anti-slavery people endorsed it. The wealthy philanthropist, the fiery abolitionist, and the Quakers, both Hicksite and Orthodox, united to advance the cause.[38]

The committee to prepare an address finally published its *Address to Abolitionists*, of which Lewis C. Gunn was the principal author. This was probably the strongest statement of the case yet issued. Gunn's fundamental premises were concise: "*The love of money is the root of the evil of slavery—and the products of slave-labor are stolen goods.*" After dwelling on the sinfulness of slaveholding and the consequent involvement of consumers in the sin,

[38] Philadelphia. Requited Labor Convention. *Minutes of Proceedings of the Requited Labor Convention, Held in Philadelphia, on the 17th and 18th of the Fifth Month, and by Adjournment on the 5th and 6th of the Ninth Month, 1838* (Philadelphia, 1838), pp. 3-13. This pamphlet also contains extracts of letters from abolitionists who were unable to attend. Among these one from William Goddell to Lewis C. Gunn, dated Utica, Aug. 29, 1838, is especially significant. He wrote: "It would give me pleasure to attend your *Free Labor Convention*. . . . In the early part of our anti-slavery movement, I was among those who anticipated some action on this subject by the societies then organized. The topic was introduced in the Convention in your city for forming the American Anti-Slavery Society, in December, 1833, when it appeared that not a few of our friends were apprehensive that its incorporation into our enterprise would cripple our efforts, and shut us out of the manufacturing districts of the North. A resolution, however, was adopted, recommending the subject to the attention of the Executive Committee. But it soon appeared that neither the members of that body, nor the constituency represented by them, were prepared to make any decisive advances in relation to it. The subject was not understood. It had not been discussed . . ." (pp. 16-18). *Pennsylvania Freeman*, Oct. 11, 1838.

he concluded that "*The purchaser of slave produce is, himself, virtually the plunderer of the slaves*. . . . And the consumers . . . are slaveholders." Replying to the objection that abstinence by a few would have no perceptible effect, he insisted "that if the use of these productions is positively assisting (in however small a degree) to keep men in slavery, no one, who considers it wrong to keep them so, is at liberty to assist even to this trifling extent." Estimating the Society of Friends at 150,000, members of anti-slavery societies at 180,000, and adding the free colored people, he reached a total of 600,000 persons "who might be expected . . . to withdraw at once their pecuniary aid" from the sin of slavery, and that "would produce *an impression* . . . on the market for slave produce, and on the profitableness of slave labor."[39]

The first annual meeting of the American Free Produce Association was held at Philadelphia on October 15 and 16, 1839, with over one hundred persons present, among whom were William Bassett and William Lloyd Garrison. The executive committee lamented its small accomplishments, but hailed emancipation in the British colonies as a great boon to the cause, and looked forward to an increase in the amount of free labor cotton when an agent could be sent to the South to seek it out. While no stores had yet been opened, the committee anticipated no trouble in getting cotton cloth manufactured. Resolutions were passed appointing a committee to lay the free labor argument before anti-slavery societies generally, to name delegates for the Anti-Slavery Convention of the World to be held at London in 1840, to correspond with the British India Society,[40] and "to prepare and publish a list of the places or countries where articles, the result of remunerated labor, are raised, or whence they can be obtained, together with a list of Stores . . .

[39] Lewis C. Gunn, *Address to Abolitionists* (Philadelphia, 1838), pp. 3-16.
[40] The British India Society was a body of social-minded men who hoped by influencing British public opinion to gain for the people of India the rights and privileges they might properly expect. For the economic advancement of India, the Society urged the abolition of protective duties so that the products of India might compete fairly with those of other parts of the Empire (*Pennsylvania Freeman*, March 24, 1841; Joseph Pease, Sen., *A Letter from Joseph Pease, Sen., Addressed to Jonathan Backhouse, of Darlington, Both Members of the South Durham British India Society, on the Subject of the Slave Trade, and Slavery*, Darlington, May 11, 1842, n.p., September 5, 1842, a broadside).

at which free goods can be purchased." William Bassett was elected president, and other changes in officers were made.[41]

The annual meeting of 1840 passed the customary resolutions in support of the boycott principle, but had to confess that comparatively little had been accomplished. Less than four hundred dollars had been raised. With this, however, a small amount of free labor cotton had been purchased and manufactured, chiefly into muslin. The list of places where free labor products could be obtained had been prepared, but was so incomplete as to be almost useless.[42] On January 29, 1841, a mid-year meeting was held. Various resolutions were passed endorsing the cause and concluding, "Resolved, That we eminently attribute the want of success in the abolition enterprise, to professed abolitionists not witnessing by their lives the truths they proclaim." The executive committee during this year did considerable work in urging the free produce cause upon anti-slavery societies generally.[43]

The third annual meeting convened at Clarkson Hall on October 19 and 20, 1841. The committee to propose a plan more effectually to promote abstinence from slave labor products reported "That they . . . were unable to see in what way the object of the Association could be better promoted than by each one abstaining from the use of slave grown produce." They did, however, recommend the raising of more funds for the purchase of newly available supplies of free labor cotton, they issued an "Address to Abolitionists," and they sent a letter to each state anti-slavery society urging adoption of the free produce principle.[44]

The Association held its fourth annual meeting on November 21, 1842. Delegates were present from the Philadelphia Female

[41] Weld-Grimké, *Letters . . . 1822-1844*, II, 797; *Liberator*, IX, 163, 182 (Oct. 11, Nov. 15, 1839). Information on the meeting is taken from Garrison's editorial summary of the proceedings. William Bassett was a shoemaker of Lynn, Mass. He was disowned by the Society of Friends in July, 1840, for his anti-slavery activities (William Bassett, *Proceedings of the Society of Friends in the Case of William Bassett*, Worcester, Mass., 1840, pp. 2-24). Bassett himself published this document in protest against the action.
[42] *Free Labor Advocate*, I, 6, 8 (Feb. 8, 1841); *Pennsylvania Freeman*, Sept. 10, 1840. This list had been compiled at the instance of the Union Free Produce Association.
[43] *Free Labor Advocate*, I, 46, 48, 200 (March 8, 24, Aug. 9, 1841); *Pennsylvania Freeman*, Feb. 17, 1841.
[44] *Free Labor Advocate*, I, 342 (Dec. 24, 1841); *Protectionist*, I, 359 f. (Dec. 4, 1841); *Pennsylvania Freeman*, Oct. 27, Nov. 3, 10, 1841.

Anti-Slavery Society, the Association of Friends for Promoting the Abolition of Slavery, etc., and from the Union Free Produce Association. The executive committee reported the wide circulation of their "Address to Abolitionists" issued in 1841. They also announced "a small paper for gratuitous circulation," the *American Free Produce Journal,* of which the first number had been issued in October, 1842. Its purpose was to spread the free produce idea among anti-slavery societies generally. The manufacturing committee reported the purchase of more cotton and the sale of about $3,000 worth of goods during the preceding year. A resolution to dissolve the Association led to an "animated discussion" and resulted in a unanimous vote to carry on.[45]

The report for 1843 was the most optimistic in the society's history. Operations had been considerably extended as a result of the increased demand and supply of free labor goods. Sale of goods was more than double that of the preceding year. Discussion of the subject and organization of free produce associations had occurred in many places, but there was still much to be done. Consequently, the society was urged "to continue its efforts with increased zeal and diligence. . . ."[46]

In 1844 the Association addressed the abolitionists of Great Britain, reviewing its activities and urging the cause generally. The executive committee continued to feel cheered with progress of the cause. New societies had been organized, and the demand for goods was increasing.[47] The executive committee in 1845 confessed that there was little to report except what properly pertained to the manufacturing committee. After referring to an increasing interest in the free labor cause, the executive committee avowed its

. . . undiminished confidence in the principles on which our Association is based, and earnestly wish that the hearty adoption of them by every Anti-Slavery Society in the land, might render unnecessary a distinct organization for their promotion . . . it is a cause of surprise and deep regret that many abolitionists whose eagle eyes are continually discovering new and rugged paths of duty . . . should

[45] *National Anti-Slavery Standard,* Nov. 17, 1842; *American Free Produce Journal,* I, 1-4 (Oct. 1, 1842). This was presumably the only issue published. No mention of it is made in the report for 1843.
[46] American Free Produce Association, *Fifth Annual Report* (Philadelphia, 1843), pp. 3-11; *Free Labor Advocate,* Jan. 5, 1844.
[47] *Free Labor Advocate,* March 22, May 10, 1845. These societies will be dealt with in the next chapter.

not yet have seen . . . that true consistency requires of them abstinence from the purchase of the ill-gotten fruits of slavery.[48]

During 1846 and 1847 the optimistic tone continued. In the latter year the American Free Produce Association ceased to manufacture cotton goods, since that function had been assumed by the Free Produce Association of Friends of Philadelphia Yearly Meeting.[49] The Association continued a nominal existence for several years, but there appear to be no records.[50] The non-Quaker minority had fallen away, having become absorbed in other more spectacular and less exacting fields of anti-slavery activity. The Quaker members, almost all, went into the new organization which was limited to members of the Society of Friends. Thus ended the first phase of the free produce movement.

[48] *Non-Slaveholder*, I, 20 (Feb., 1846).

[49] *Ibid.*, I, 161 (Nov., 1846); *Free Labor Advocate*, Nov. 18, 1847; Free Produce Association of Friends of Philadelphia Yearly Meeting, Minutes of the Board of Managers (MS), Dec. 8, 1847, p. 71.

[50] As late as 1852 George W. Taylor still had on hand in his free produce store some 200 yards of cloth and some other articles which had been turned over to him in 1847, but remained "unsold because they would not sell at the prices he was authorized to sell them at—" On Nov. 16, 1852, he turned them over to Rebecca S. Hart, "by order of Danl. L. Miller, Jr. Treasurer of the Assn." (G. W. Taylor to Rebecca S. Hart, Nov. 16, 1852, Taylor Letterbooks, I, 74).

CHAPTER III

FREE PRODUCE BECOMES A QUAKER MOVEMENT

Before 1831 the anti-slavery movement was a mild-mannered, theoretical reform sponsored by small and isolated groups of plain people. Its chief manifestation was in manumission societies which flourished in the South even more than in the North. Quakers were responsible for the manumission societies of North Carolina and Tennessee, while in Kentucky Baptists and Methodists had similar organizations. Propaganda was limited and local in extent, gradual emancipation was the goal, and funds scarcely existed. Benjamin Lundy was the leader of this movement in which most Quakers participated. Fanaticism in the hands of William Lloyd Garrison, Theodore Dwight Weld, Henry B. Stanton, and other crusaders put an end to the old movement, which could show little in actual results. The new abolition was grounded on the crusading spirit, evangelism, constant agitation, immediate emancipation, political action, and no compromise.

Since all these characteristics did not appear at the outset, the abolition movement was looked upon with favor by a very considerable portion of the Society of Friends. Between 1831 and 1837, especially, most Quakers of liberal views were extremely active in forming the new state anti-slavery societies, while the most radical often belonged to a half-dozen local and regional organizations. It was not long, however, before the new abolition movement showed characteristics which were not compatible with Quaker views. The introduction of other reforms, such as temperance, women's rights, and political action against slavery, resulted only in hostility and withdrawal by the large body of conservative Quakers who felt it wrong to engage in the "excitements of the day." Liberal and radical Quakers, however, could not see any dangerous tendencies, and so continued their anti-slavery work.

With these differences of opinion rife in American Quakerdom, trouble was bound to follow. By 1836 some of the yearly meetings openly endorsed the doctrine of immediate emancipation and condemned colonization.[1] During the next three years the conserva-

[1] *Friend* (Philadelphia), X, 46 (Nov. 12, 1836). The unit of organi-

tives gained control of nearly every yearly meeting and proceeded to issue minutes of advice warning members against joining "mixed" anti-slavery societies.[2] In many places, especially in the West, Quaker meetinghouses were closed to abolition lecturers through the caution or hostility of conservative leaders.[3]

The results were various. Throughout the East conservative power was too strong to be disputed, so that there was no united protest. Some radical members withdrew voluntarily, some were disowned, others remained members in name though "fellowship" was strained; while still others quietly formed free produce societies to satisfy their anti-slavery convictions, otherwise participating in their religious organization and bearing quietly various discriminations against them, particularly refusal to permit the use of meetinghouses for their free produce meetings.[4] Adding to these complica-

---

zation in the Society of Friends is the yearly meeting, which assembles annually. The fifteen Orthodox and seven Hicksite yearly meetings in America are all independent of each other. A Permanent Board (originally called the Meeting for Sufferings) acts for the yearly meeting between sessions. Each yearly meeting is divided into quarterly meetings which assemble three or four times a year. Below them are the monthly meetings which are the business sessions of congregations. Subordinate to monthly meetings are preparative meetings, usually composed of one congregation. In all these units business is conducted by secretaries, clerks, and committees. These and other Quaker organizations have no president, nor do they vote on questions before the house; rather the clerk records "the sense of the meeting."

[2] The term "mixed" was regularly used to refer to any group composed of Quakers and non-Quakers. Indiana Yearly Meeting (Orthodox), *Minutes* (1838), pp. 18 f., (1839), p. 24; *Friend* (Philadelphia), XII, 279 (June 1, 1839); George Evans to Mary Evans, March 19, April 23, May 27, 28, 1840 (Letters from George Evans to His Family and Particular Friends . . . [MS]).

[3] Indiana Yearly Meeting (Orthodox), *Minutes* (1841), p. 17; *Anti-Slavery Bugle* (Salem, Ohio), Sept. 5, 1845.

[4] Among the most prominent of those who withdrew voluntarily were Elizabeth Buffum Chace and Abby Kelley. Outstanding among those disowned were Arnold Buffum, Charles Marriott, Isaac Tatem Hopper, James S. Gibbons, and George F. White, all of the Hicksite branch, and William Bassett. The grounds for expulsion were usually vague and seldom mentioned the real cause. Conspicuous among those who remained nominal members was Lucretia Mott, while to the last category belong almost all the members of free produce societies in the East. See Thomas Edward Drake, "Northern Quakers and Slavery" (MS doctoral dissertation, Yale, 1933), pp. 213-215, 218; William Bassett, *Proceedings of the Society of Friends in the Case of William Bassett*, pp. 2-24; "A Testimony of the Monthly Meeting of New York, concerning our Beloved Friend, George F. White, deceased," in New York Yearly Meeting (Hicksite), *Memorials concerning*

tions was the Wilbur-Gurney controversy, which troubled the Society for many years following 1845. The difficulty was partly doctrinal, but it also had social manifestations. Joseph John Gurney (1788-1847), a well-educated British Friend of cultured tastes, promulgated views of an evangelical nature. American opposition to him was led by John Wilbur (1774-1856), a Rhode Island Quaker who believed in traditional doctrines and viewpoints. Gurney's visit to the United States resulted in a separation in New England, where Wilbur led the minority of seceders. This event caused repercussions throughout all the yearly meetings. Separation in Ohio did not come until 1854, when the majority went with the Wilburites. Three general conferences to promote unity were unsuccessful. While there was no actual separation in Philadelphia Yearly Meeting, the situation was long unhappy. In the end those of Wilburite leanings concentrated at Fourth and Arch Street meetinghouse, while those who favored Gurney centered at Twelfth Street meeting. Members of this latter meeting led the free produce movement and other reforms in Philadelphia. Those of Wilburite tendencies held aloof from social questions and politics.[5]

In the West there was less peace and more action. The trouble centered in Indiana Yearly Meeting, where there was a large minority of radicals. Advices in 1839 against joining anti-slavery societies were spurned by one quarterly meeting.[6] Leadership in the yearly meeting was about equally divided between radicals and conservatives. The trouble reached a climax in October, 1842, when the conservatives seized control and removed from the Meeting for Sufferings (the executive board of the yearly meeting) eight members of long standing. These included Charles Osborn, a distinguished and revered minister and anti-slavery leader; Benjamin Stanton and Henry H. Way, editors of the *Free Labor Advocate and Anti-Slavery Chronicle;* and others of equal prominence. This action put the yearly meeting into a furor which lasted for months.

Deceased Friends, published by Direction of the Yearly Meeting of New York (New York, 1859), pp. 161-177; Lydia Maria Child, *Isaac T. Hopper: A True Life* (Boston, 1853), pp. 388-399.

[5] Allen C. Thomas and Richard Henry Thomas, *A History of the Friends in America* (6th ed., Philadelphia, 1930), pp. 144-148, and information given the writer by Francis R. Taylor. The literature of this controversy is very extensive. The Hicksite branch was not affected.

[6] *Friend* (Philadelphia), XVII, 85 (Dec. 9, 1843).

In February, 1843, after much discussion the radical faction determined to secede and organized itself as Indiana Yearly Meeting of Anti-Slavery Friends.[7]

Indiana Yearly Meeting of Anti-Slavery Friends soon had between two and three thousand members. Its center was Newport (now Fountain City), Indiana, which was the home of Levi Coffin and a prominent station on the Underground Railroad. The *Free Labor Advocate* became the press organ of the seceders who sought, but never received, recognition by any other yearly meeting. In 1845 a mission of five British Friends from London Yearly Meeting sought to reconcile the two factions, but failed completely.[8] Indiana Yearly Meeting of Anti-Slavery Friends continued to function until 1857, when it dissolved for want of members, most of whom had gone back to their original yearly meeting. No formal disownments or reinstatements ever took place. Meanwhile Indiana Yearly Meeting tacitly acknowledged its mistake in pursuing a policy which had resulted in such a separation, and became itself progressively abolitionist. Indeed, in 1850 the question came up in the Committee on the Concerns of the People of Color, whereupon a spontaneous desire for a special meeting on free produce became apparent. Such a meeting was held with some fifteen hundred persons in attendance, and the subject was fully discussed. When the ques-

[7] The chief sources on this controversy are: Indiana Yearly Meeting of Anti-Slavery Friends, Minutes (MS), 1843-57, and the *Free Labor Advocate and Anti-Slavery Chronicle* (1841-48). All Quaker periodicals both in America and in the British Isles carried some account of it. Walter Edgerton's *History of the Separation in Indiana Yearly Meeting of Friends* . . . (Cincinnati, 1856) is a contemporary account by the Clerk of Indiana Yearly Meeting of Anti-Slavery Friends. Though biased, it contains most of the documents and recriminatory tracts issued by both sides. A secondary account is given in Ruth Anna Ketring, *Charles Osborn in the Anti-Slavery Movement*, Ohio Historical Collections, Vol. VII (Columbus: The Ohio State Archaeological and Historical Society, 1937), pp. 50-84.

Walter Edgerton (1806-1879) was born in eastern Ohio, and moved to Indiana during his childhood. He was one of the leading radicals in Indiana Yearly Meeting. In later years he was disowned for issuing a pamphlet, *Ancient and Modern Quakerism*, which dwelt on the inconsistency of practice with doctrines. Edgerton then joined the Progressive Friends.

[8] The situation of Indiana Yearly Meeting of Anti-Slavery Friends was similar to that of an insurgent government which cannot obtain diplomatic recognition. Other yearly meetings refused to receive documents or communitions from the Anti-Slavery Friends; hence the latter had no opportunity even to present their arguments.

tion of organizing arose, it was determined to leave that to local units.[9]

While Indiana Yearly Meeting of Anti-Slavery Friends existed as an organized body, they gave much attention to the free labor principle. Each yearly meeting received full reports on the subject from all subordinate meetings. Even so, they were beset by many difficulties and found it necessary each year to appoint special committees to deal with offenders. In 1847 they issued an "Epistle to all those who desire the abolition of Slavery, wherever located." In 1849 the boycott of slave labor products was made a required article of discipline, in a more determined effort to remedy individual shortcomings.[10] These Anti-Slavery Friends were the only organized body of Quakers who ever so recognized the free labor principle. Despite all these measures, "deficiencies" in the boycott were reported each year. These led in 1853 and again in 1855 to an "Epistle of Advice to Quarterly and Monthly Meetings, and Friends Individually."[11]

Friends of the Hicksite branch in the Philadelphia area attempted with some success to reach a compromise which would please all. When the yearly meeting in 1837 saw fit to take no action on the slavery question, those most interested formed the Association of Friends for Promoting the Abolition of Slavery, and Improving the Condition of the Free People of Colour, with a particular view to drawing in those who felt it wrong to join "mixed" societies. Although this was not wholly successful in satisfying the most radical, yet the society continued active for at least fifteen years. This Hicksite organization was not strictly a free produce association, but in 1838 it published *An Address to the Members of the Religious Society of Friends, on the Propriety of Abstaining from the Use of the Produce of Slave Labour,* which urged Friends to investigate the question and consider whether it must not inevitably become a part of their testi-

[9] Levi Coffin to Samuel Rhoads, Newport, Ind., Oct. 30, 1845 (G. W. Taylor MSS); *Friends' Review*, IV, 89 f. (Oct. 26, 1850).

[10] Indiana Yearly Meeting of Anti-Slavery Friends, Minutes (MS) (1849), p. 247. The revised Query read as follows: "Are Friends careful to bear a faithful testimony against Slavery, avoiding the practice of giving their suffrages, or influence for the elevation of slaveholders or proslavery men to public offices, and carefully endeavoring to abstain from the productions of the unpaid toil of the Slave, and do they likewise bear a faithful testimony against all other prize goods?"

[11] Indiana Yearly Meeting of Anti-Slavery Friends, Minutes (MS) (1853), pp. 317-321; (1855), pp. 341, 342, 346.

mony against slavery. Another tract, *An Appeal to Females of the North, on the Subject of Slavery,* by a "Female of Vermont," was issued the same year, while in 1840 the Association's Committee on Requited Labor addressed members on the boycott principle. In 1843 the Society appealed to Friends generally and also adverted to dissensions over the matter of joining "mixed" societies.[12]

The report for 1847 reviewed the Association's decade of existence, dwelt earnestly on the subject of free produce, mentioned memorials sent to Congress, and recorded the maintenance of a school for colored women. The report for 1849 explained that "We have not been unmindful of the subject of Free Produce, although few opportunities for action in relation to it have presented themselves." During the next two years they admitted "no active measures" in the matter, but continued to stress its importance.[13]

Orthodox Friends as such formed their first free produce association in 1845. A year earlier Samuel Rhoads issued a tract entitled *Considerations on the Use of the Productions of Slavery, Addressed to the Religious Society of Friends.* He prefaced his argument by observing that

. . . *as a body,* the Society has not yet adopted abstinence from the produce of slave labor as one of its testimonies.

Believing that the *principles* of the Society, faithfully and consistently carried out, would lead to this abstinence, the compiler has felt constrained to offer the following . . . to the calm, serious, and unprejudiced attention of his fellow-members.

He reviewed all the arguments from the time of Woolman onward and adverted to the hostility of the conservative faction in the following manner:

[12] The Association of Friends for Advocating the Cause of the Slave and Improving the Condition of the Free People of Color, *An Address to the Members of the Religious Society of Friends on the Propriety of Abstaining from the Use of the Produce of Slave Labour* (Philadelphia, 1838), pp. 3-11; ———, *An Appeal to the Females of the North, on the Subject of Slavery.* By a Female of Vermont . . . , republished by the Association . . . (Philadelphia, 1838), p. 7; ———, *An Address to the Members of the Society of Friends* . . . (Philadelphia, 1843), pp. 3-12; *Pennsylvania Freeman,* Sept. 17, 1840. Charter members totaled 121.

[13] Association of Friends for Promoting the Abolition of Slavery, and Improving the Condition of the Free People of Color, *Annual Report* . . . (Philadelphia, 1849), pp. 6 f.; *Annual Report . . . for the Year 1850,* pp. 14-18; *Annual Report . . . for the Year 1851,* p. 4.

We are told that we shall have no reward for attempting *to do good in our own wills:* and it is most uncharitably assumed that those who are labouring in this cause are so doing. Would it not be well to inquire what our reward will be for persisting *to do evil in our own wills*. . . .[14]

With this impetus a few Philadelphia Friends met on April 24, 1845, considered the subject again, "Proposed to form an association within the limits of Philadelphia Yearly Meeting for the special purpose of promoting and encouraging the production, by free labour, of the articles which are generally procured from servile hands," appointed a committee to prepare a constitution, and issued a call to Friends generally to meet on June 20, 1845. Thirty responded and organized the Free Produce Association of Friends of Philadelphia Yearly Meeting. Another meeting was held on September 19, when the constitution was further considered and organization was completed. The constitution provided that membership was to be confined to the Society of Friends, that meetings should be annual, that officers were to be a secretary, treasurer, and board of managers, that the association should procure information toward obtaining a supply of free labor goods and should correspond with other such associations, and that a fund should be raised by contributions and by loans without interest to purchase and manufacture free labor cotton.[15] The first officers were: Secretary, George W. Taylor; Treasurer, Samuel Alsop; Managers, Enoch Lewis, Abraham L. Pennock, Edward Garrett, Samuel Rhoads, Elihu Pickering, Israel H. Johnson, Samuel Allinson, and Thomas Wistar, Jr.[16] The Board of Managers immediately set about their duties as detailed in the constitution.

The first annual meeting of the Association was held on April 21, 1846, at Clarkson Hall, while Philadelphia Yearly Meeting was

[14] Samuel Rhoads, *Considerations on the Use of the Productions of Slavery, Addressed to the Religious Society of Friends* (2d ed., Philadelphia, 1845), pp. 2, 27. Conservatives believed that those Friends who were most active in the anti-slavery cause had not waited for divine guidance.

[15] Free Produce Association of Friends of Philadelphia Yearly Meeting, *Circular to Our Fellow Members of the Religious Society of Friends* (Philadelphia, Sept. 3, 1845), a broadside; *Non-Slaveholder*, I, 6-10 (Jan., 1846). The constitution was also published in the *Free Labor Advocate*, Oct. 11, 1845. Henceforth citation will be: Philadelphia Free Produce Association, the name as adopted in 1848.

[16] Philadelphia Free Produce Association, Minutes of the Board of Managers (MS), Sept. 20, 1845, p. 1.

in session. A large audience attended the proceedings, which were dominated by the report of the Board of Managers. Although only seven months had elapsed since operations actually got under way, the Managers had wide activities to report. They had concentrated on means of obtaining free labor cotton and felt assured of a reliable supply in the future. The manufacture of 10,000 yards of cloth had been contracted for, and some progress had been made in finding supplies of other free labor products. They looked forward to the early establishment of a free produce store. An address entitled *On the Duty of Abstaining from the Productions of Slave Labour, Especially in Reference to the Destruction of Human Life Which Slavery Occasions* had been prepared and five thousand copies circulated.[17]

When the second annual meeting occurred on April 20, 1847, the prospect looked encouraging. New free produce associations had been formed in various parts of the country, and several stores were in operation. The demand for free labor cotton goods exceeded the supply. Some 60,000 yards of cloth had been manufactured, and sales thereof during the year had amounted to about $5,500. It was determined to hold meetings of the Association more frequently; hence the next meeting was set for June 11, 1847. Because of insufficient announcement attendance was small, but members went away "edified and refreshed."[18]

One of the chief activities during 1847 was the employment of an agent to facilitate and increase the supply of free labor cotton. Progress was also reported in the search for such other products as rice and sugar. Because suspicion among customers was hampering the sale of free labor goods, the Association gave repeated assurances that its goods were absolutely untouched by slave labor. The constitution was amended to provide for semiannual meetings, the first of which was set for October 16, 1847.[19]

On March 17, 1848, the Managers authorized a change of name to the Philadelphia Free Produce Association of Friends.[20] During

[17] Philadelphia Free Produce Association, Minutes of the Board of Managers, pp. 37-47; *Non-Slaveholder*, I, 64-68 (April, 1846).

[18] *Non-Slaveholder*, II, 96-101, 222 (May, Oct., 1847).

[19] Philadelphia Free Produce Association, Minutes of the Board of Managers, May 17, 1847, pp. 68 ff. These minutes do not contain, for the most part, the reports of the Board to the annual and semiannual meetings. *Non-Slaveholder*, II, 7, July, 1847; III, 75 ff., 238, April, Oct., 1848; *Friends Review*, I, 531 f., May 13, 1848.

[20] Minutes of the Board of Managers, March 20, 1848, p. 78.

1848 an agent was again employed to procure cotton. Manufacture of cotton cloth increased in quantity and improved in quality. As to the free produce cause, the Managers were "led to believe that Friends in many places within the limit of the five Northern Yearly Meetings are more and more awaking to the conviction that this testimony must be taken up and faithfully borne." The question of slavery as a whole, however, was gloomily viewed, since the Mexican War and the trend of public agitation appeared to Friends to show a decided pro-slavery tendency.[21]

Attendance at the annual meetings both in 1849 and 1850 declined because of conservative disapproval. While annual meetings were always held during yearly meeting week, it was never possible to hold them in the same building, nor could public notice be given in yearly meeting sessions. In October, 1848, the Board of Managers had turned over most of its business transactions to George W. Taylor, who had since 1847 been operating the free produce store in Philadelphia. Committee management in the procuring and manufacture of cotton and other free labor goods had not proved entirely satisfactory; hence it was considered best to place the responsibility upon a single individual.[22] Henceforth the Managers confined their activities to "the advocacy of the principles of our cause, and the collection of useful information upon the subject. . . ." In pursuance thereof they had "prepared and circulated an *Address to the Members of the Religious Society of Friends on the Subject of Slavery and the Slave Trade.*" The procurement and manufacture of cotton were proceeding as formerly, and the establishment of new societies showed progress in the cause. Four Friends' boarding schools were now regularly supplied with free labor groceries, and some sheeting was being manufactured for Haverford dormitories.[23]

The Compromise of 1850 and the accompanying violent agitation of the slavery question were heavy blows to the abolition cause. No report of the Philadelphia Free Produce Association for 1851 appears to have survived. The meeting was held on April 22, but the *Non-Slaveholder* had suspended publication in December,

[21] *Non-Slaveholder*, IV, 97 ff., 106 (May, 1849).
[22] Philadelphia Free Produce Association, Minutes of the Board of Managers, Oct. 9, 1848, p. 80.
[23] *Non-Slaveholder*, V, 97 f., 103 (May, 1850). The schools were Moses Brown (R. I.), Nine Partners (N. Y.), Haverford and Westtown (Pa.).

1850, and the sympathetic *Friends' Review* carried only the briefest notice of the meeting.[24]

By 1852 the paralyzing effects of the Compromise had begun to disappear and the Philadelphia Free Produce Association, while confessing that its "efforts . . . have not been productive of any very obvious results," still expressed the "confiding hope, that they may compose one of those little rills which, widening and deepening . . . will . . . compose a river which shall sweep away this . . . frowning monument of . . . barbarism. . . ."[25] The report of 1853 reverted to a detailed explanation of the difficulties in obtaining free labor goods.[26] The numbers of those supporting the free labor principle seemed in 1854 to be increasing, but the difficulties of supplying cotton cloth were also growing. Hence it was proposed to establish a small manufacturing plant to be supervised by George W. Taylor, provided friends of the cause would subscribe fifteen thousand dollars to finance it.[27] During 1853 and 1854 the *Non-Slaveholder* was revived and published in smaller form and at a cheaper price. There appears to be no record of any meeting in 1855, though it is probable that one was held. A meeting was announced for April 22, 1856, but there is no further report.[28]

During 1854 and 1855 efforts were initiated to rejuvenate the free produce movement. As early as 1853 Henry Miles of Monkton, Vermont, proposed the forming of a national association at both the New York and Philadelphia meetings. The idea did not make much progress until Elihu Burritt took hold of it in 1855.[29] He was joined by others of the faithful in Philadelphia and New York, and in January, 1856, their campaign got under

[24] *Friends' Review*, IV, 553 (May 17, 1851).
[25] *Ibid.*, V, 555 (May 15, 1852).
[26] *Ibid.*, VI, 634 f. (June 18, 1853).
[27] *Ibid.*, VII, 533 f. (May 6, 1854); *Non-Slaveholder*, II, 47 f. (May, 1854).
[28] *Friends' Review*, IX, 506 (April 19, 1856).
[29] Henry Miles to Edmund Fry, Nov. 16, 1853 (Henry Miles MSS). For further comment on Miles see pp. 46 f., *Burritt's Citizen of the World*, I, 29 (Feb., 1855). Elihu Burritt (Dec. 8, 1810-March 6, 1879), "the learned Blacksmith," was born in New Britain, Conn., received a meager education, and after the death of his father learned blacksmithing. His eager mind and great gift for languages enabled him to master a vast amount of knowledge. He soon became interested in all kinds of reforms and worked for them alternately with his trade by which he supported himself. "Ocean Penny Postage," peace, and slavery were the questions to which he gave greatest attention (Elihu Burritt, *The Learned Blacksmith: The Letters and Journals of Elihu Burritt*, ed. Merle Curti, New York, 1937, *passim*).

way. Its chief features were the organization of a society on a broader basis, energetic efforts to increase the supply of free labor produce by offering premiums, and an attempt to prove to Southerners that free labor would be more economical. The first was carried into effect on February 15, 1856, when the North American Free Labor Produce Association was formed. In an effort to widen the base, membership was open to anyone who would pay annual dues of at least one dollar. Some non-Quakers apparently participated, and a vigorous beginning was made. Burritt, like Benjamin Lundy, was a tireless reformer. He was an energetic organizer and could rouse enthusiasm in others, but his staying power was not always great. At any moment he might become absorbed in another of the various reforms which he sponsored. A president and other officers were elected and the constitution was adopted on April 14, 1856. Soon an explanatory circular was issued, and the first annual meeting was set for the following October. In August the organization was still waiting for funds. The October meeting was not held, and apathy killed the whole effort.[30]

While Philadelphia Yearly Meeting (Orthodox) completely ignored the free produce issue,[31] the situation in New York Yearly Meeting was different. The general subject of slavery came before the Orthodox yearly meeting in 1837, when Scipio Quarterly Meeting brought it up and a special committee was appointed by the yearly meeting to survey the question. In 1838 the whole situa-

[30] *Burritt's Citizen of the World*, II, 11, 16, 45, 57, 72-75, 92 f., 122 (Jan.-Aug., 1856).

[31] The closest Philadelphia Yearly Meeting (Orthodox) came to an official pronouncement on the subject was in the "Minute on Slavery" issued by the Meeting for Sufferings in 1839, which declared: "The close connexion and intimate intercourse which is maintained between the different sections of our common country, through the diversified and widely spread channels of commerce and business, may, unless we are very watchful, blunt our sensibilities to the cruelties of slavery, and diminish our abhorrence of its injustice. We wish tenderly to incite our dear friends to an individual inquiry, . . . how far they are clear in these respects; and should such an examination awaken serious apprehensions as to any part of their traffic, that they may be willing to forego every prospect of gain, arising from the prosecution of business, which is incompatible with the purity of our religious profession" (*Minute on Slavery*, a broadside, reprinted from the Minutes, April 15-19, 1839). Philadelphia Yearly Meeting (Hicksite) in 1838 considered revising the annual query on slavery to include questioning on the use of slave labor produce, but decided against the change (*Friends' Intelligencer*, I, 33, May 1, 1838).

tion was thoroughly canvassed and the committee was continued. The next year they reported that

the Yearly Meeting recommended to our members, to embrace every right opening to maintain and exalt our righteous testimony against Slavery; and where any of our members feel any religious scruples as to the use of the products of slave labor, that they faithfully attend thereto. . . .[32]

Free labor sentiment was especially strong in Farmington Quarterly Meeting, which in 1842 addressed its monthly meetings and members generally on the subject. It urged all "to adhere singly to their duty" in avoiding "the fruit of slavery . . . though we may have to pay a higher price. . . . The sacrifice we may thus have to make . . . will . . . bring a blessing greater than that of the increase of earthly treasure." This address was much used in later advocacy of the cause. Further attention was given the subject the next year, when the women's meeting made a lengthy report. In later years the subject was adverted to, both by the Orthodox and Hicksite branches, but never so forcefully as in 1842.[33]

The radical element in New York Yearly Meeting (Orthodox) actively entered the cause simultaneously with the Philadelphia group. At the yearly meeting session in 1845 the Meeting for Sufferings produced an "Essay" on the "subject of freely using and trading in articles produced by the labor of slaves . . ." and concluded that "If . . . *it is the market for Slave produce which makes Slavery*, we must feel that it is a serious matter to be customers in this market."[34] Thereupon the Free Produce Association of Friends of New York Yearly Meeting was formed, almost identical in organization with the Philadelphia society. The first annual meeting on May 27, 1846, was publicly announced in yearly meeting session

---

[32] New York Yearly Meeting (Orthodox), *Address of Scipio Quarterly Meeting* [Cayuga Co.] *on the Subject of Slavery, to Its Members* (Skaneateles, N. Y. [, 1837]), p. 11; *Friends' Intelligencer*, I, 33, 65 (May 1, June 1, 1838); *Pennsylvania Freeman*, June 7, 1838.

[33] New York Yearly Meeting (Orthodox), *Address of Farmington Quarterly Meeting to the Monthly Meetings Constituting It, and to the Members of the Same Generally* (Mount Pleasant, Ohio, 1850), pp. 1-8. (This was a republication by the Board of Managers of the Free Produce Association of Friends of Ohio Yearly Meeting.) New York Yearly Meeting (Hicksite), *Minutes*, May 24, 1851, pp. 9 f., June 2, 1854, pp. 12 f.; *Friends' Review*, VII, 683 (July 8, 1854).

[34] *Non-Slaveholder*, I, 17, 23 (Feb., 1846). The entire "Essay" is printed in the *Friends' Review*, III, 237-240 (Dec. 29, 1849).

and so had a large attendance. The Board of Managers had held six meetings during the year, and had been chiefly engaged in searching for supplies of free labor products. Their report dwelt on the need for a large adherence to the free produce principle in order to bring a supply of goods onto the market at reasonable prices. The constitution had been printed and circulated. Only small progress had been made in raising funds to open a store.[35]

The meeting of 1847 was endorsed by several prominent members of the yearly meeting. Efforts were concentrated on raising additional funds for the opening of a store. During the next year this project got under way and was announced at the large annual meeting of 1848. Within the yearly meeting itself two special sessions on slavery and "the disuse of slave produce" were held, and the Meeting for Sufferings issued another minute.[36]

The report of 1849 opened with the lament "that little progress had been made. . . ." George Wood and Lindley M. Hoag asked to be relieved of the free produce store which up to August, 1848, had netted them nothing but trouble and losses. The business was transferred to Robert Lindley Murray at a loss of 25 per cent on the capital investment. As a means of promoting information on the free produce cause the Managers had subscribed to fifty copies of the *Non-Slaveholder*. The greatest need of the Association was additional funds.[37]

This continued to be the case in 1850, when the Managers were chagrined to report that only eighty-five dollars had been contributed that year. Neither was the store prospering; indeed, suspension seemed likely unless patronage increased. The printing of a series of free labor tracts, in co-operation with the Ohio association, was contemplated but not yet undertaken.[38]

[35] *Non-Slaveholder*, I, 97 (July, 1846); Free Produce Association of Friends of New York Yearly Meeting, [Address] To the Managers of the Free Produce Association of Friends of Philadelphia Yearly Meeting, New York City, June 30, 1846 (G. W. Taylor MSS).

[36] *Non-Slaveholder*, III, 128, 149 f. (June, July, 1848); *Friends' Review*, I, 548 f. (May 20, 1848). The report for 1847 was not published (L. B. Parsons to G. W. Taylor, Flushing, N. Y., Aug. 5, 1847, G. W. Taylor MSS). At the yearly meeting $550 was raised, and local committees were appointed to continue the work of raising funds.

[37] Free Produce Association of Friends of New York Yearly Meeting, *Report of the Board of Managers . . . Adopted at the Annual Meeting of the Association, Held Fifth Month, 29, 1849* (New York, 1849), pp. 1-8.

[38] Free Produce Association of Friends of New York Yearly Meeting, *Report of the Board of Managers . . . Adopted at the Annual Meeting of*

The situation of the society continued to be equally gloomy throughout 1851; the store did not prosper and deliveries of free labor cotton to Liverpool did not come up to expectations. The Managers felt, however, that the free labor cause as a whole was advancing. The work in England was being pressed with vigor, and the culture of cotton by free labor appeared to be expanding in various parts of the world.[39] To assist the store a broadside appeal reviewing once more the free labor cause and urging Friends to patronize the free labor store was published, while the yearly meeting itself again recommended the subject to general attention.[40]

This appeal did no good, however, and so in February, 1852, R. L. Murray informed the Managers that he could not continue the store. It was taken over by his foreman, Ezra Towne, who combined a general grocery business with the free labor enterprise which he undertook to maintain. The Managers supplied two thousand dollars in capital to help finance the free produce branch of the business. During this year the Managers issued a tract entitled *Slavery and the Slave Trade—Who Is Responsible*, which they hoped was "doing a silent work of good."[41]

While the free labor movement, wrote the Managers in 1853, seems "to be gaining strength and courage, not only abroad, but in distant sections of our own country; it is painful and humiliating to be obliged to chronicle among ourselves, an apparent decline of interest in this deeply interesting and important cause." The store continued to operate, but additional difficulties in obtaining goods were experienced. As in each previous report, the Managers reviewed possible sources of cotton supply and adverted to the Association's responsibility in furnishing it to spinners and weavers.[42]

During 1854 the Managers helped to sustain the *Non-Slave-*

---

the Association, Held Fifth Month, 28th, 1850 (New York, 1850), pp. 1-12. This report also contains the constitution and a list of members totaling 88.

[39] Free Produce Association of Friends of New York Yearly Meeting, *Report of the Board of Managers . . . Adopted at the Annual Meeting of the Association, Held Fifth Month, 27th, 1851* (New York, 1851), pp. 1-6.

[40] Free Produce Association of Friends of New-York Yearly Meeting, [circular addressed to members, New York, 1851, a broadside]; New York Yearly Meeting (Orthodox), *Minutes*, May 28, 30, 1851, pp. 9, 21.

[41] Free Produce Association of Friends of New York Yearly Meeting, *Report of the Board of Managers . . .* (New York, 1852), pp. 1-12. The tract referred to has not been seen by the writer.

[42] Free Produce Association of Friends of New York Yearly Meeting, *Report of the Board of Managers . . .* (New York, 1853), pp. 1-8.

holder by subscribing for fifty copies. The free produce store was slightly more prosperous, and an effort to raise a "Guarantee Fund, for facilitating the shipment of Free Labor Cotton to England" netted $145.00.[43] The yearly meeting again gave attention to the movement when at the instance of Westbury Quarterly Meeting, a statement setting forth the official attitude was prepared and sent to all subordinate meetings.[44] The report of 1855 was presented "under feelings of more than usual discouragement. . . ." The "Guarantee Fund" had amounted only to half the needed sum, and "the same sad apathy continued. . . ." The Managers had issued a new tract, and the store continued in its usual manner.[45] On this gloomy note the records of the New York Free Produce Association cease forever. While the organization may have lived a year or two longer, it is unlikely that any more reports were published. The New York society was never so strong as that in Philadelphia, and in fact acted more as an auxiliary. Even so it was second in importance in the East.[46]

Out in western New York a small group of Hicksite Friends were active in the free produce cause as early as 1831. Then or later they formed the Western New York Free Produce Association. Its history is unknown except for the fact that it existed in 1842. At that time its leaders proposed to publish the *Friend of Freedom, and Free Labor Advocate*. This journal was probably issued, for a short time at least, under the supervision of Levi Taft and Lorenzo Mabbett. In 1845 Mabbett issued the following prospectus for the *Champion of Freedom:*

A Monthly sheet, devoted to the FREE PRODUCE enterprise, and Industrial Association, is again to be resumed. . . . It should be borne in mind, that *this periodical is the first, and (as yet) the only one in the world whose main feature is the application of the abstinence principle to the products of slave labor.*

LORENZO MABBETT

[43] Free Produce Association of Friends of New York Yearly Meeting, *Report of the Board of Managers* . . . (New York, 1854), pp. 1-8.
[44] New York Yearly Meeting (Orthodox), *Minutes* (1854), pp. 12 f., 17 f.; *Friends' Review*, VII, 683 (July 8, 1854).
[45] Free Produce Association of Friends of New York Yearly Meeting, *Report of the Board of Managers* . . . (New York, 1855), pp. 1-8.
[46] In 1856 George W. Taylor wrote, "I reluctantly give up all hope of aid . . . from the New York Friends, who so strongly recommend the subject [of free produce] from year to year . . ." (G. W. Taylor to R. L. Murray, July 16, 1856, Taylor Letterbooks, II, 314).

Lorenzo Mabbett was one of the most active abolitionists among radical Quakers. Wherever he went, a free produce society was sure to appear. His earlier activities centered around Sodus Bay. About 1848 he moved farther west, to Collins Center, New York, where he organized the Free Produce Association of Collins and Its Vicinity. This society was active for at least the next three years in raising funds, supporting the *Non-Slaveholder*, and obtaining a supply of free labor goods.[47]

Before turning to the West, it may be well to survey the remaining minor and local free produce societies in the East. In New England the movement did not get under way until 1848. A "very numerous meeting of Friends" was held on June 14 of that year in Newport, Rhode Island, at which the whole cause was opened up and thoroughly discussed. In place of a formal organization, committees in each quarterly and monthly meeting were appointed to advance the cause in their own localities, canvass the demand for free labor goods, and see that such goods were available for sale in suitable places.[48] At the meeting in 1849 considerable progress was reported in supplying free labor goods to stores in several towns. The committee system of operation was continued for another year. Faith in the cause was renewed at the meeting of June 18, 1850, when visiting Friends from Philadelphia and New York reviewed all the arguments for abstinence. The committee arrangement was continued, and the meeting "after a free and harmonious expression of sentiment," adjourned to convene the next year.[49] A large audience in 1851 heard reports from all the local committees, showing "that exertions have been made to some extent" in promoting the free labor cause. The committees in 1852 reported ten localities scattered throughout the yearly meeting area where free labor dry goods and groceries could be obtained.

[47] *National Anti-Slavery Standard* (New York), Nov. 17, 1842, March 6, Aug. 7, 1845; Elizabeth Margaret Chandler, *Poetical Works . . . with a Memoir of Her Life and Character*, by Benjamin Lundy (Philadelphia, 1836), p. 40; Lorenzo Mabbett to G. W. Taylor, Collins Center, N. Y., Aug. 30, 1848 (G. W. Taylor MSS); *Non-Slaveholder*, V, 77 f. (April, 1850). The radicals in this area broke away in 1848 and formed North Collins Yearly Meeting, affiliated with the Progressive Friends.

[48] *Free Labor Advocate*, July 14, 1848; *British Friend* (Glasgow), VI (Aug. 31, 1848); *Non-Slaveholder*, III, 172 f. (Aug., 1848).

[49] *Non-Slaveholder*, IV, 193 f. (Sept., 1849); *Friends' Review*, III, 714 f. (July 27, 1850); Free Produce Association of Friends of New England Yearly Meeting, *Free Produce Meeting* (Newport, R. I., June 18, 1850, a broadside).

The meeting of that year adopted a pledge obligating those who signed it to promote the use of free labor goods "by providing, when they can be obtained, such articles for ourselves and the consumption of our families; and by encouraging their use by others."[50]

There were at least two local free produce societies in New England. The first of these, the Free Produce Association of Western Vermont, was chiefly the work of one man, Henry Miles. As an active abolitionist he wrote voluminously for the local newspapers on many phases of the slavery question. He was secretary of the Anti-Slavery Society of Ferrisburgh and Vicinity, formed in 1835.[51] In 1839 he, as chairman of a committee of Friends, was asking, "Do not we . . . virtually give . . . our support to the slaveholder . . . as often as we use or deal in the product of the unpaid toil of the slave?" Miles was ever anxious to work in the free produce cause, but being isolated in the Vermont countryside with only a small number of other Quakers, he was considerably handicapped. In 1846 he made a journey to Virginia to investigate possible sources of free labor products. In 1853 he attended the meeting of the New York Free Produce Association, and in 1854 he was anxious to go to Texas as agent of the Philadelphia association. Henry Miles, more than anyone else, was responsible for the idea of a national free produce movement, which was embodied in Elihu Burritt's North American Free Labor Produce Association.[52]

[50] Free Produce Association of Friends of New England Yearly Meeting, [*Minutes,*] June 16, 1851 (a broadside); Minutes of Free Produce Meeting 6 mo 17. 1852 at Newport (MS); [*Pledge*], June 17, 1852 (a broadside).

[51] Henry Miles (1795-June 9, 1885) was born in Kent County, England, and became a member of the Society of Friends in 1816. He was married in 1818 to Mary Hagen, and in 1832 they with their seven children came to America. After a short residence in Montreal the family settled in Addison County, Vt., where they engaged in farming. Miles had extensive scientific interests, especially in the field of geology. He was also much concerned with education and various social reforms, while at the same time he wrote extensively on doctrinal questions and Biblical interpretation (Henry Miles MSS, *passim; Friends' Review,* XXXVIII, 745, June 27, 1885; Hamilton Child, comp., *Gazetteer and Business Directory of Addison County, Vt., for 1881-82,* Syracuse, N. Y., 1882, p. 160).

[52] Minutes of Ferrisburgh Monthly Meeting, May, 1839; Henry Miles to Elihu Burritt, Nov. 4, 1846; Henry Miles to G. C. Sampson, June 11, 1853; Henry Miles to Edmund Fry, Nov. 16, 1853; Henry Miles to George W. Taylor, Aug. 3, Dec. 10, 1854; Henry Miles to Levi Coffin, Feb. 1, 1855 (Henry Miles MSS). Most of the Henry Miles manuscripts are at Harvard College Library; a fragment is at Duke University Library. Those at Harvard consist largely of articles and essays on a variety of subjects. This material is fragmentary and most of it is undated, making it very difficult to

THE FREE PRODUCE MOVEMENT 47

Certainly Miles was responsible for the Free Produce Association of Friends in Ferrisburgh Monthly Meeting. Unfortunately his draft of the constitution of this society bears no date, but it was almost certainly founded between 1845 and 1853. No other records have survived. About 1854 it was presumably expanded into the Free Produce Association of Western Vermont. At the end of a year this society still had no board of managers; hence Miles took upon himself the writing of the first annual report, which was a polemic on slavery in general and a discussion of the free produce movement in particular. It closed with an appeal to form a national free produce association which should raise money, send out lecturers and tracts, form local associations, enlist the women, and appeal to nonslaveholding planters.[53] Here ends the free produce record in Vermont. In 1855 there existed a Free Labor Association at Manchester, Maine, whose members were "very earnest and active in the movement" and were "doing much to enlighten the public mind. . . ." Their activities beyond 1857 are unrecorded.[54]

The most unexpected appearance of free produce activity came in 1849 at North Carolina Yearly Meeting. Enoch Lewis, who was present, gave an account of the circumstance: ". . . before the meeting actually adjourned, some of their own members made a proposal, that a meeting should be held to consider the subject of the use of Free Produce." Two meetings in fact were held, at both of which Enoch Lewis and others spoke in behalf of the free produce cause. Much interest was aroused, and committees were appointed in the monthly meetings to correspond with each other on the means of obtaining free labor produce. They adjourned to meet the next year, but whether they did is unrecorded.[55] In any case the excitement of the Compromise debates resulted in the following advice in 1851: ". . . it is our duty to be a law-abiding people, and in no wise improperly to interfere in the relation between master and slave, or with any of the commotions or excitements of

---

use. Some letters are dated. *Voice of Freedom* (Montpelier, Vt.), May 18, 25, June 29, 1839, Feb. 29, 1840.

[53] [Free Produce Association of Western Vermont,] First Annual Report (Henry Miles MSS, Duke University). Internal evidence indicates the date as 1855. The entire document is in Henry Miles's handwriting.

[54] *Friends' Review*, IX, 90-92 (Oct. 20, 1855); *Burritt's Citizen of the World*, II, 45 (March, 1856).

[55] *Non-Slaveholder*, IV, 271 f. (Dec., 1849); *Friends' Review*, III, 183 (Dec. 8, 1849).

the day arising therefrom. . . ." But the subject was not forgotten, at least not by New Garden Quarterly Meeting, which announced that

... this meeting was brought into deep feeling on the subject of Friends using the products of Slave labour, and after a time of weighty deliberation thereon, it was thought best to lay the subject before the Yearly Meeting for its consideration.

This led to "a free expression of sentiment thereon," but the subject was deferred until next yearly meeting for further consideration.[56] When the subject came up in 1852, it was fully discussed and "it was with much unanimity agreed that the meeting could not take any action on the subject; yet Friends were encouraged to attend, in their individual capacity, to what may appear to be required of them."[57] This apparently brought to an end the free produce movement among North Carolina Friends.

In the West the free produce movement was more vociferous but smaller in accomplishment. In general it got under way a little earlier in the West than in the East. On September 6, 1842, the Marion County Free Produce Association was formed at Whetstone, Ohio. The brief constitution pledged members to abstain as much as possible from the use of slave labor products and not to be deterred by pecuniary considerations. Membership was not restricted to the Society of Friends. C. K. Lindley, a merchant at Mount Gilead, undertook to keep a stock of free labor goods.[58]

In Wayne County, Indiana, the movement got under way even earlier. The large Quaker population, many of them radicals, was responsible for the activity in this area. Indiana Yearly Meeting itself took some action in 1840, when its Committee on the Concerns of the People of Color investigated the means of obtaining free labor goods. Their report, made in 1841, was staunchly backed by New Garden Quarterly Meeting, which added its own strong appeal on the need for abstinence and for making it a required testimony.[59] The first District Convention of Indiana Abolitionists, held near Economy (Wayne County) on November 10 and 11,

[56] *Friends' Review*, V, 195 f. (Dec. 13, 1851).
[57] *Ibid.*, VI, 153 f. (Nov. 20, 1852).
[58] *Free Labor Advocate*, Nov. 5, 1842. One of the officers was Daniel Osborn, a son of Charles Osborn. How long this society continued active is not recorded.
[59] Walter Edgerton, *History of the Separation*, pp. 43-47. New Garden Quarterly Meeting contained a large proportion of radicals.

1840, passed a resolution endorsing free labor and recommending that merchants "supply us with goods of that description, as far as practicable." As dissension increased between conservative and radical Friends on how far they should go in the anti-slavery movement, the radicals made a compromise move by offering to form an anti-slavery society limited to Quakers. To this end they held a convention at Newport, Indiana, on January 11, 1841, where the subject of free produce "was very fully considered," the principle was endorsed, and its adoption urged. As a concession by the radicals, however, the meeting was not a success. Nothing daunted, they held a second convention on September 14, 1841, at Spiceland, Indiana, and projected a larger gathering for yearly meeting week. That was cut short by the hostile conservatives in Indiana Yearly Meeting, who hastily clamped down on any such willful notions. The radicals waited a few months and held their convention on January 22, 1842, at Newport. Here sixty-five Friends, assembled in the Methodist church, organized the Wayne County Free Produce Association. They undertook to boycott slave labor products, to induce merchants to provide free labor goods, and not to be deterred by "pecuniary considerations."[60] Among the officers were Benjamin Stanton and Henry H. Way, the two editors of the *Free Labor Advocate*, Levi Coffin, Jonathan Unthank, Jacob Grave, and other prominent radicals who led in the formation of Indiana Yearly Meeting of Anti-Slavery Friends. In April, 1842, the society took the first steps toward establishing a mercantile firm to supply free labor goods throughout the West.[61]

With the same nucleus of leaders, but on a somewhat broader basis, the Western Free Produce Association was organized at a Friends' meetinghouse in Union County, Indiana, on February 14, 1842. Actual operations were postponed until local meetings could further discuss all angles. Officers of all anti-slavery societies throughout Ohio, Indiana, Illinois, Michigan, and Iowa were asked to hold meetings for discussion of the free labor principle.[62]

The first efforts to obtain a supply of free labor goods were hampered by the serious business depression of 1842, but enthusiastic

---

[60] *Protectionist*, I, 7 ff., 58 (Jan. 1, Feb. 16, 1841); *Free Labor Advocate*, I, 16 (Feb. 8, 1841), March 2, 1842.

[61] *Free Labor Advocate*, I, 207, 368, 379 (Aug. 9, 1841, Jan. 8, 27, April 30, 1842).

[62] *Ibid.*, Feb. 23, 1842; *National Anti-Slavery Standard*, June 30, Nov. 17, 1842.

Westerners hoped this difficulty would soon be overcome. Several persons in various localities expected to handle such goods, and all looked forward to the time when a wholesale store in Cincinnati would supply the whole region.

The first annual convention of the Western Free Produce Association was held at Green Plain (Clark County, Ohio), on August 8, 1842. It was a large and enthusiastic assemblage. Reporting it, Aaron L. Benedict wrote:

Ministers of various denominations, lawyers, judges, and statesmen, were present, and gave their hearty sanction to our principles and measures. At this meeting a resolution was passed, making the "Western Free Produce Society" auxiliary to the American; and the executive committee was directed to appoint delegates to attend the anniversary of the latter. . . . A committee was appointed to devise means for establishing a wholesale free-labor store in Cincinnati. It is proposed to be done by joint stock investments. Hon. Thomas Morris offered to invest his whole capital in such an establishment.

It was believed that the American Free Produce Association could supply the goods needed, thereby relieving the infant Western association of the burdens of manufacturing. A committee was appointed to raise funds, while the executive committee urged the formation of auxiliary societies in each county.[63]

The second anniversay meeting, on August 25, 1843, at Greensboro, Indiana, had little progress to report. During the year at least one local convention at Salem, Union County, Indiana, had reorganized the Salem Free Produce Association by removing the restriction which limited membership to Quakers.[64] Indiana Yearly Meeting of Anti-Slavery Friends tried to keep the movement going by scheduling six local conventions. Enthusiasm was on the wane, however, partly because of the difficulty in getting free labor goods, the lack of funds, and the want of experienced leadership. Though

---

[63] *National Anti-Slavery Standard*, Nov. 18, 1842; *Free Labor Advocate*, Feb. 23, March 2, April 16, Aug. 27, Sept. 3, 1842. Thomas Morris (1776-1844), a self-educated man, settled near Cincinnati in 1795. He was admitted to the bar in 1804, but soon entered politics, serving in the Ohio legislature, 1813-33, and in the U. S. Senate, 1833-39. As Senator he antagonized his colleagues and his constituents by his unyielding abolitionism. Obviously, nothing came of his grandiose offer, mentioned above.

Aaron Lancaster Benedict was a resident of Morrow County, Ohio. He was later a leader in the Alum Creek Free Produce Association.

[64] *Free Labor Advocate*, Oct. 15, 1842, Dec. 6, 1843, Feb. 2, 1844.

the officers failed to attend the meeting of 1844, the assemblage listened to a member's account of his tour of Alabama, and then renewed their pledge to abstain from the products of slave labor. There was probably no meeting in 1845.[65]

Meanwhile the Salem Free Produce Association, led by William Beard (1788-1873), had kept a spark of life, and in 1846 he took the initiative in calling a convention to meet at Salem, Union County, Indiana, on October 10. At that meeting Henry H. Way "moved that we now proceed to reorganize the Western Free Produce Association." After much discussion the motion was adopted "nearly unanimously." The convention resolved that it was a duty to abstain entirely from slave labor products, that it was necessary to establish a wholesale house in Cincinnati, and that subscriptions should be opened to raise three thousand dollars for that purpose. A year later only four hundred dollars had been raised, and so the meeting of 1847 simply continued activities of the preceding year.[66]

The convention of 1846 had selected Levi Coffin as the proper person to open the wholesale business in Cincinnati. Coffin declined on both financial and personal grounds. But further search revealed no one so well qualified by experience and inclination for the work, and so Coffin yielded and began business at Cincinnati in April, 1847.[67] During the next year the Executive Committee called three general meetings at various places to raise additional funds, which had already been pledged, to help finance Coffin.[68] During 1848 he purchased seven thousand dollars worth of cotton goods from the Philadelphia Free Produce Association, besides what he had manufactured locally. Less than half the three thousand dollars was raised and so something else had to be done. Accordingly, a convention was held at Salem, Union County, Indiana, on November 19, 1850, to form a joint stock company. It was incorporated as the Western Manufacturing Company, and books were opened. Unfortunately not enough shares were taken to permit the charter to become operative, and so Coffin struggled on as best he could with his limited capital until 1857, when he sold out the business and returned

[65] *Ibid.*, Sept. 8, 1843, Feb. 22, 1845; Levi Coffin to Samuel Rhoads, Newport, Ind., Oct. 30, 1845 (G. W. Taylor MSS).
[66] *Free Labor Advocate*, Aug. 15, Nov. 7, 1846, Nov. 18, 1847; *Non-Slaveholder*, II, 12, 276 (Jan., Dec., 1847).
[67] Levi Coffin, *Reminiscences*, pp. 265-272; *National Anti-Slavery Standard*, Sept. 24, 1846.
[68] *Free Labor Advocate*, March 9, 1848.

to his old home at Newport.[69] Records of the Western Free Produce Association, incomplete at best, do not go beyond 1848.

While the free produce associations in Indiana and western Ohio were operating in spasmodic attacks of enthusiasm followed by periods of lethargy, friends of the cause in eastern Ohio were pursuing a steadier and more successful course. The first meeting was held at Mount Pleasant, Ohio, on September 11, 1846, when the Free Produce Association of Friends of Ohio Yearly Meeting was organized by the adoption of a constitution. Another meeting held on November 21 completed the organization and signed up twenty additional members. The constitution was modeled on that of the Philadelphia association, and membership was limited to the Society of Friends. While the new society was composed chiefly of Orthodox Friends, the Hicksite branch of Ohio Yearly Meeting in 1847 gave official attention to the subject of abstinence and issued "An Address of the Yearly Meeting on Slavery."[70]

Initial activities of the Board of Managers were confined to a search for supplies of free labor goods and to an effort to raise funds. During the next two years "circumstances beyond the control" of either Managers or members prevented any annual meetings. These circumstances were the Wilbur-Gurney controversy, which rent Ohio Friends for the next six years and finally resulted in a separation in 1854. Meanwhile the Board of Managers continued to meet. Their chief accomplishment was the formation on June 6, 1848, of the Mount Pleasant Free Produce Company. To finance it, 250 shares at ten dollars each were sold, and a free produce store was opened at Mount Pleasant a short time later.[71]

The first annual meeting of the Association was held on September 4, 1849, when the Managers announced that the store had been in operation more than a year and that the cause was advancing throughout the country. Their optimism was borne out by the acces-

[69] Levi Coffin, *Reminiscences*, pp. 292-295; *Non-Slaveholder*, IV, 13 f. (Jan., 1849); *Western Friend* (Cincinnati), I, 418 f. (Dec. 7, 1848). The panic of 1857 may have been a deciding influence in Coffin's retirement at this time.

[70] *Non-Slaveholder*, I, 153 (Oct., 1846).; Free Produce Association of Friends of Ohio Yearly Meeting, Minutes of the Board of Managers (MS), Sept. 11, Nov. 21, 1846 [no paging]; Ohio Yearly Meeting (Hicksite), *Minutes, 1847* . . . (Salem, Ohio, 1847), pp. 11 f.

[71] Free Produce Association of Friends of Ohio Yearly Meeting, Minutes of the Board of Managers, March 6, 1847, Jan. 29, March 19, 20, June 6, 1848.

sion of thirty-five new members.[72] During that autumn the Managers turned their attention to the publication of tracts, which was to become their primary activity in later years. The committee to select suitable material presented nine pieces, chiefly articles which had appeared in the *Non-Slaveholder*. Of these, six were chosen for publication. By the spring of 1850 tracts totaling forty-eight pages in editions of one thousand copies were ready for distribution.[73] The cost of printing was $44.30, which had been raised by contributions.

The annual meeting on September 3, 1850, was one of the best ever held by the Association. Over two hundred Friends attended, and a considerable addition to the membership was made. Committees for each monthly meeting were appointed to ascertain the extent of free labor sentiment and the number willing to purchase free labor products, and to report to the annual meeting in 1851. Several visiting Friends renewed enthusiasm by vigorous speeches in behalf of the cause. The Managers reported their issuance of forty-six thousand pages of tracts and explained their as yet unsuccessful efforts to co-operate with the Eastern societies in this phase of the work. They reviewed the status of the free labor cause throughout this country and in Britain as well. Evidences of

[72] Ohio Free Produce Association, Minutes of the Board of Managers, Sept. 5, 1849. (For the sake of brevity citation will be in this form.) *Non-Slaveholder*, IV, 217 ff. (Oct., 1849).

[73] Ohio Free Produce Association, Minutes of the Board of Managers, Oct. 13, Nov. 16, 1849, Feb. 2, Aug. 21, 1850. The tracts published were listed as follows:
  [1] Louis Taber, "Considerations on abstinence from the use of the products of slave labor: Addressed to the Members of Ohio Yearly Meeting" (8 pp.).
  [2] Enoch Lewis, "Observations on slavery and the slave trade & the methods of extinguishing them" (10 pp.).
  [3] "Extracts from the Letters of Nathan Thomas written from the South while acting as the agent of the Philadelphia Free Produce Association of Friends" (12 pp.).
  [4] "Address of the Farmington Quarterly Meeting, New York; to the monthly meetings constituting it and to the members of the same generally, combined with the Address of New York Yearly Meeting" (8 pp.).
  [5] "Extracts from the Address of the British and Foreign Anti-Slavery Society to the Friends of the Anti-Slavery cause on the disuse of slave labor produce" (4 pp.).
  [6] "Stolen goods; or the gains of oppression," by le Mabbett [probably Lozenzo Mabbett] and "A Comparison of stolen goods with slave labor produce, by Elihu Burritt" (4 pp.). The second, third, fourth, and fifth are reprints from the *Non-Slaveholder*.

dissension among Friends on slavery appear throughout this report, but the Managers were convinced that Friends everywhere would soon come to see the duty of abstinence; meanwhile each one should strive to do his "whole duty toward our oppressed fellow-men, so that even those who may look with coldness or indifference upon our exertions, witnessing our sacrifices and sincerity, may be constrained to say, 'let them alone, they have done what they could.' "[74]

During 1851 the Managers corresponded with leaders in other parts of the country and issued two more tracts, the "Plea of Necessity and an original article by E. Cattell." Feeling that the cause was handicapped by the demise of the *Non-Slaveholder* at the end of 1850, the Managers began a movement to revive it and appointed a committee to raise one hundred dollars for that purpose.[75]

At the annual meeting on September 9, 1851, the Managers lamented that they had been "able to accomplish much less . . . than would have been desirable." They had published the report and proceedings of the meeting of 1850 together with the society's constitution in an edition of one thousand copies and were issuing a new edition of the first tract published. They reviewed the general status of the cause and put the question of reviving the *Non-Slaveholder* to the society as a whole, though nothing came of it at this time. Consequently, the Managers made preparations in 1852 to publish a periodical in Ohio to be devoted to the free produce cause, in lieu of the *Non-Slaveholder*. Material was prepared for the first issue and a prospectus issued when the magnitude of the undertaking appeared too great for the available finances, and so the project was suspended but not abandoned. At the annual meeting of 1852 it was thoroughly discussed, and again an effort was launched to raise money.[76] The autumn was chiefly occupied with

---

[74] Ohio Free Produce Association, Minutes of the Board of Managers, Sept. 3, Oct. 12, 1850; ———, *Extracts from the Minutes of the Annual Meeting of the Free Produce Association of Ohio Yearly Meeting. Held 3d of Ninth Month, 1850, with the Report of the Board of Managers. Constitution, &c.* (Mount Pleasant, Ohio, 1851), pp. 1-16. This was issued as No. 7 in the series of tracts. *Friends' Review*, IV, 54 (Oct. 12, 1850).

[75] Ohio Free Produce Association, Minutes of the Board of Managers, Jan. 11, Feb. 8, April 12, Sept. 3, 1851; *The Plea of Necessity* (Mount Pleasant, Ohio, 1851), pp. 1-12. There is no further clue to the "original article" by Ezra Cattell.

[76] Ohio Free Produce Association, *Second Annual Report of the Board of Managers . . . Held 9th of Ninth Month, 1851* (Mount Pleasant, Ohio,

completing negotiations by which the *Non-Slaveholder* was revived in January, 1853, the Ohio association acting as guarantors to the extent of two hundred dollars. The Managers were very active in pushing subscriptions and so far succeeded that the journal paid expenses during 1853.[77]

The annual meeting of 1853 received reports from various localities and continued the local committees for another year. Membership at this time stood at one hundred and fifty. They also continued their support of the *Non-Slaveholder*.[78] In December, 1853, it was agreed that each member of the Board of Managers should furnish at least two articles a year for that journal, and write at least two letters, with a view to advancing the cause. In January, 1854, twenty dollars were appropriated for publishing tracts, cards, mottoes, one-leaf circulars, and other propaganda. The cards and circulars were distributed in May, and a new edition of two earlier tracts was authorized.[79]

When the annual meeting assembled on September 4, 1854, it was "not without feelings of encouragement, that the labors of our Association have not been in vain, that the Managers again bring forward their annual report." They felt that this year had seen the greatest advancement in the cause yet observed. They were especially heartened by the fact that at "Oberlin Collegiate Institute" the free produce "testimony has been embraced by most of the faculty and students, and will thus be disseminated throughout the land, by the most extensive, earnest, and powerful agency." Henry Miles's and Elihu Burritt's initial efforts in New York to form a national free produce association were a piece of "gratifying intelligence." The latter half of the report was devoted to the gloomy side of the picture—the continued apathy of many Friends, the

---

1851), pp. 1-8. This report is also in the MS Minutes of the Board of Managers. For some reason this was called the second annual report, although there had been reports in 1849 and 1850. ————, Minutes of the Board of Managers, Oct. 12, Nov. 22, 1851, Feb. 7, March 13, July 10, Aug. 14, Sept. 6, 1852; *Friends' Review*, V, 26 (Sept. 27, 1851).

[77] Ohio Free Produce Association, Minutes of the Board of Managers, Sept. 11, Oct. 9, 1852, Jan. 8, Feb. 12, March 12, May 14, June 11, Aug. 13, 1853.

[78] Ohio Free Produce Association, Minutes of the Board of Managers, Sept. 5, 1853; *Non-Slaveholder*, I, N.S., 11, 89 (Feb., Nov., 1853).

[79] Ohio Free Produce Association, Minutes of the Board of Managers, Oct. 8, Nov. 12, Dec. 12, 1853; Jan. 14, Feb. 10, March 3, May 13, June 10, Aug 12, 1854.

Fugitive Slave Law, and the constant difficulty in procuring free labor goods.[80]

During 1855 the Managers were largely occupied with preparing articles for publication and with promoting subscriptions to *Burritt's Citizen of the World*, which succeeded the now permanently defunct *Non-Slaveholder*. At the annual meeting of September 5, 1855, the Managers continued to be hopeful of a better supply of free labor goods, especially now that George W. Taylor's mill was in operation. In furthering discussion of the free labor cause, they announced that "efforts have been made to enlist the services of several anti-slavery periodicals, whose editors were thought to be favorable to the cause."[81] The Society continued through 1859, but there was little constructive activity. In the latter year the Managers issued "An Address on the Use of Slave-Labor Products." The accounts and daybooks of the Mount Pleasant Free Produce Company continue as late as 1863.

Although the Ohio association was never very successful in building up auxiliary societies, one group deserves brief mention. It was the Alum Creek Free Produce Association, located in Morrow County, Ohio, and formed in 1852 under the leadership of Griffith Levering. It was furnished with tracts and other material by the Ohio association. The old anti-slavery center of Salem, Ohio, was also active in carrying on local work.[82] In 1859 Indiana and Ohio Yearly Meetings (Orthodox) both recommended that individual members should "attend faithfully" to any scruples they felt about using slave labor products.[83]

It remains to glance at the farthest Western point which the free produce movement reached. As early as 1841 Friends in Iowa met and organized, on February 6, the Salem Anti-Slavery Society, with thirty members. The matter of free labor was discussed, the

[80] Ohio Free Produce Association, Minutes of the Board of Managers, Sept. 4, 1854; *Non-Slaveholder*, II, N.S., 73-75 (Sept., 1854); *Friends' Review*, VIII, 154 f. (Nov. 18, 1854).

[81] Ohio Free Produce Association, Minutes of the Board of Managers, Sept. 5, 1855; *Friends' Review*, IX, 90-92 (Oct. 20, 1855).

[82] Ohio Free Produce Association, Minutes of the Board of Managers, Sept. 11, 1852, Sept. 5, 1853, Oct. 13, Nov. 11, 1855; *Non-Slaveholder*, I, N.S., 111 (Feb., 1853); *Friends' Review*, XII, 821 ff. (Sept. 3, 1859). Griffith Levering (1818-1873) was a native of Maryland, where he first took part in anti-slavery work.

[83] Ohio Yearly Meeting (Orthodox), *Minutes* (1859), p. 8; *Friends' Review*, XIII, 88 (Oct. 15, 1859).

annual report of the American Free Produce Association was read, and the whole subject was turned over to the executive committee for further attention. Late in 1846 a free produce society was formed, but it was probably short-lived. The subject came up again when, on March 29, 1850, those interested assembled in the Friends' meetinghouse at Salem (Henry County), Iowa, to consider "what practical measures" they could adopt "to encourage the use of free products." They passed resolutions endorsing abstinence and appointed a committee "to procure the names of those who are willing to pledge themselves to patronize a free labor store. . . ." A store was opened in 1850, and in 1861 a store existed, but whether it was the same establishment in continuous operation, is doubtful.[84]

Finally some mention of the free produce movement in Great Britain is requisite.[85] Though the evidence is very sketchy, it appears that some of the British societies working during the 1820's for emancipation in the British colonies, endorsed the boycott idea. Two of these were the Tropical Free Labor Company and the Female Society for the Relief of British Negro Slaves.[86] Individual English Friends, like Joseph Sturge, were active before 1840 in the free produce movement, but there was presumably no kind of Quaker organization before 1847. The subject was discussed in both "World" anti-slavery conventions at London in 1840 and 1843. Late in 1846 Elihu Burritt expressed his determination to "commence a public agitation" on the subject as soon as he could receive sufficient information about free labor products from the Philadelphia Free Produce Association.[87] The first meeting, held on January 29, 1847, discussed methods of promoting the use of free labor products. At London Yearly Meeting that year Joseph Sturge

[84] *Pennsylvania Freeman*, March 24, 1841; *Non-Slaveholder*, II, 97 (May, 1847); V, 100 (May, 1850); *Friends' Review*, XV, 184 (Nov. 23, 1861). At this date Joseph Steer was operating a store near Iowa City.

[85] Since the sources are fragmentary at best, no attempt has been made to give a complete account.

[86] *Genius of Universal Emancipation*, VII, 2, 85 (July 4, Sept. 15, 1827).

[87] Elihu Burritt to [Samuel Rhoads], Exeter, England, Sept. 29, 1846 (G. W. Taylor MSS); *Free Labor Advocate*, Feb. 23, 1846. Joseph Sturge (1793-1859) was very active in promoting emancipation in the British colonies. In 1837 he visited the West Indies for the purpose of ascertaining the real condition of the Negroes there. His report was influential in repealing the apprenticeship system which had been set up by the original emancipation act. Sturge visited the United States in 1841, where American Friends gave him a not entirely cordial reception because many of them disagreed with his advanced views on slavery and other questions.

pressed the matter, and Samuel Rhoads went to England for the purpose of presenting to British Friends the operations and needs of the Philadelphia Free Produce Association.[88] London and Newcastle-on-Tyne were the two centers of the British movement. During 1848 the Ladies' Newcastle Free Produce Association was formed. The next year was signalized by efforts to secure the manufacture of goods from free labor cotton. In this attempt Josias F. Browne, a manufacturer of Manchester, was most prominent. The momentum generated by these efforts resulted in a large and enthusiastic meeting on May 31, 1849, which was addressed by all the leaders of the cause.[89] Agitation for the establishment of a "Free-labor warehouse" did not have any tangible results until 1851, when such a store was established in Manchester. By this time there were twenty-six free produce societies in Britain, and at Newcastle an active press was publishing numerous tracts and a periodical entitled *The Slave*.[90] A store was opened by Bessie Inglis in London in 1853, and continued at least through 1856. The large meeting in 1853 was addressed by Calvin Ellis Stowe and Harriet Beecher Stowe as well as numerous British leaders of the cause. Great optimism was expressed, especially if sufficient money could be raised to finance adequately the effort to obtain large supplies of free labor goods.[91] Further accounts of the British movement are not available.

This survey of free produce societies gives some idea of their extent and nature. Between 1826 and 1856 twenty-six societies were formed in the United States. These thirty years may be subdivided into three distinct periods of activity. The first, 1826-37, was dominated by the Free Produce Society of Pennsylvania, and included five other bodies in the Philadelphia area and three in eastern Ohio. The second period covers the years 1838-44, when the work was carried on by the American Free Produce Associa-

---

[88] *Free Labor Advocate*, March 25, 1847; *Western Friend*, I, 3 (Nov. 11, 1847); *Non-Slaveholder*, II 90 (April, 1847); Philadelphia Free Produce Association, Minutes of the Board of Managers, May 17, 1847, p. 64; Samuel Rhoads to G. W. Taylor, Aug. 30, 1847 (G. W. Taylor MSS).

[89] *Non-Slaveholder*, III, 123 (June, 1848); IV, 137 f. (June, 1849); *Friend* (London), VII, 117 (June, 1849); *Friends' Review*, II, 702 f. (July 21, 1849).

[90] Free Produce Association of Friends of New York Yearly Meeting, *Report of the Board of Managers* (1851), p. 4. See also Chapter VI.

[91] *British Friend* (Glasgow), IX, 172, 180 (July 1, 1853); Burritt's *Citizen of the World*, II, 78 (May, 1856).

tion. This time many prominent abolitionists espoused the free produce cause, and it appeared that the boycott idea might become a major factor in the abolition crusade. When that anticipation failed to materialize, the boycott on an organized basis was left to the Quakers, who adopted it as the form of anti-slavery protest least objectionable to their more conservative fellow-members. Between 1845 and 1856 there were eleven free produce associations formed which limited their membership to Quakers. Most important was the Free Produce Association of Friends of Philadelphia Yearly Meeting. The New York and New England associations were the other larger bodies in the East. In the West organization began in 1842 with the Western Free Produce Association and the Free Produce Association of Friends of Ohio Yearly Meeting leading the work. The remaining societies, both east and west, were more local in nature and for the most part auxiliary to some larger body.

The free produce societies never had strong financial support. There was never money to be spent on lecturers, and although considerable printed propaganda was issued, it reached only a limited audience, composed chiefly of Quakers. There was never money to buy free labor cotton in quantities; hence the amount of cloth made from such cotton was limited in extent and variety. Quakers who supported the cause did not have the funds to develop it into a large movement, and the idea was not compelling enough to attract outsiders.

CHAPTER IV

THE SEARCH FOR FREE LABOR PRODUCTS

During the thirty years of organized free labor work, activity centered in the search for supplies of free labor products and in making them available to adherents of the movement. When refusal to use slave labor goods was confined to a few individuals, those persons were forced to abandon the use of cotton cloth, cane sugar, rice, and coffee if they carried out their conscientious scruple. When the movement reached the stage of organization, however, the case was different. The chief purpose of organization was not to abandon the use of cotton, sugar, rice, and coffee, but to find areas where these products were raised by free labor and to bring them into the market.

Benjamin Lundy was probably the first individual to undertake a systematic search of this kind. The American Convention of 1827 had its attention called to the subject by the Wilmington (Delaware) Society for the Encouragement of Free Labor and the Pennsylvania Free Produce Society, both of which reported their initial efforts. The latter issued a circular questionnaire, the results of which, however, are not available. With these beginnings the American Convention appointed a committee, headed by Lundy, to continue the investigation.[1] He and others optimistically believed that they could obtain free labor cotton, sugar, and coffee from Haiti, while coffee could also be had from Santo Domingo, Java, and LaGuayra, and Canton sugar was available for a price.[2]

The first efforts to obtain cotton, however, were confined to the United States. As early as 1828 Charles Collins of New York was receiving a few bales of cotton from one Francis Williamson of Murfreesboro, North Carolina. This was manufactured into "Pittsburgh cord," drilled, fine, plaid, and coarse shirtings, and printed muslins, priced from nineteen to twenty-one cents per yard.[3]

[1] American Convention . . . , *Minutes* (1827), pp. 3 ff., 40 f., 46; *Genius of Universal Emancipation*, VII, 11 (July 14, 1827).
[2] *Genius of Universal Emancipation*, VI, 8 (Sept. 16, 1826). LaGuayra was the chief seaport of Venezuela. Legislation was passed in 1821 which emancipated at birth the children of slave parents. Slavery was not entirely abolished in Venezuela, however, until 1854. Sugar from this area was generally considered to be the product of free labor.
[3] *Genius of Universal Emancipation*, VIII, 22 f. (Jan. 26, 1828). The

Lundy's report to the American Convention in 1828 showed only limited success in his search. Coffee could be had from Haiti and some parts of South America, but for cotton nonslaveholding farmers in the Southern States seemed to be the chief source of supply. Tobacco, he reported, could easily be obtained from Ohio, or even from Canada, where it was cultivated by Negroes.[4] A committee of the Pennsylvania Free Produce Society, in answering an inquiry on the subject, gave an elaborate summary of available sources for free labor products. They had to admit that within the United States maple sugar was the only source of free labor sugar, the supply of cotton was limited and scattered, while rice was so scarce that a premium of twenty dollars had been offered for five to ten casks. They recapitulated the prospect for obtaining supplies from the East Indies and mentioned the favorable outlook in a few of the West Indian islands.[5]

In 1829, when the Female Society for the Encouragement of Free Labor was most active, it made further efforts to obtain free labor cotton. The supply came chiefly from Nathan Hunt, Jr., of Guilford County, North Carolina, who obtained it from Quaker and other nonslaveholding farmers. Some of it Hunt himself picked, and in all cases he gave an unconditional guarantee that it was the product of free labor. At least forty or fifty bales were purchased in the course of two years and manufactured into cloth for Philadelphia patrons. The varieties of goods included "Vigonia Cassimere," drilling, bedticking, canton flannel, table diaper, furniture and apron checks, shirting, sheeting, and calico.[6] Even in the West a beginning was made when C. W. Starr opened a spinning mill at Richmond, Indiana, "in which *Free Labor Cotton* alone is employed." For want of power looms, however, the yarn could not be woven in that region.[7] During these years cotton was widely grown for home consumption in southern Illinois, and some was raised in southern Ohio. This was C. W. Starr's source of free labor cotton. Abolitionists' high hopes for a good supply of free

---

higher price was justified by explaining that "the goods are much stouter, and generally contain about 1-3 more yarn than similar goods in the market."

[4] *American Convention* . . . , *Minutes* (Adjourned Session, 1828), pp. 25 ff.

[5] *Liberator*, I, 93 f. (June 11, 1831).

[6] *Genius of Universal Emancipation*, XI, 9, 43, 73 (April, June, Aug. 19, 1830).

[7] *Ibid.*, XI, 73 (Aug., 1830).

labor cotton from these areas were shattered when growing on a commercial scale failed to develop.[8]

In 1830-31 the Female Free Produce Society received about thirty bales of North Carolina cotton, two bales from South Carolina, and "a small amount" from Santo Domingo. It was manufactured into canton flannel, sheeting, shirting, and dimity. The Pennsylvania Free Produce Society reported that Charles Pierce had sold, during 1830 and part of 1831, over $5,300 worth of free labor goods, in addition to that sold by other free produce stores in Philadelphia, New York, and Wilmington, Delaware. Among his wares Pierce listed Puerto Rico, Calcutta, Canton, East Indian, and maple sugars; Puerto Rico, East India, and maple molasses; Santo Domingo and Java coffees, chocolate from Santo Domingo, cotton batting made from North Carolina cotton, and "Spanish, half-Spanish & common segars, smoking & chewing tobacco, manufactured from St. Domingo, Ohio, Connecticut and Kentucky Tobacco."[9]

Emancipation in the British West Indies was the great spur in a renewed effort to obtain free labor goods, especially foods.[10] As to cotton, the American Free Produce Association followed the practice of its forerunners and sought a supply within the United States. They found that "in consequence of the very trifling demand for free cotton in years past . . . the few who had been . . . raising it have become discouraged, and almost entirely abandoned its culture." This situation induced them to offer, through their agent in North Carolina, one cent more per pound than the market price. The committee succeeded (1841) in getting 1,378 pounds of cotton in North Carolina, for which they paid twelve cents per pound, had it manufactured, and ended with a loss of $22.21 3-4 on

[8] *Ibid.*, VIII, 46, 73 (Feb. 28, 1828, Aug., 1830); Arthur Clinton Boggess, *The Settlement of Illinois, 1778-1830*, Chicago Historical Society's Collection, Vol. V (Chicago, 1908), p. 167.
[9] *Genius of Universal Emancipation*, XI, 11, 194 (April supplement, May, 1831); *Liberator*, I, 88 (May 28, 1831).
[10] The act abolishing slavery in the British colonies was passed in 1833. It provided for immediate emancipation of children under the age of six, but established a period of apprenticeship for all others. This feature was abolished in 1837. Thereafter the free labor adherents could conscientiously use West Indian products (American Free Produce Association, notice of first annual meeting, Sept. 17, 1839; Weld-Grimké, *Letters . . . 1822-1844*, II, 797).

the whole transaction. Their hopes, however, were pinned on the growth of cotton in British India and in Texas.[11]

As the American Free Produce Association grew more active in manufacturing, the supply of goods in Philadelphia expanded somewhat. In 1842 their wholesale agent was J. Miller McKim,[12] while Lydia White continued the retail business. They advertised ginghams, canton flannel, and muslin in several qualities, table diaper, bird eye towels, buff pantaloon stripes, cotton batting, bed-ticking, calicoes, stockings, knitting cotton, lampwicks, and other articles.[13] Most of these goods were made from one thousand dollars worth of "free Texas cotton" which the Association received at the end of 1841. Early in 1843 business had improved so that they were able to reduce prices 10 per cent. This was in part due to the opening of several new stores in the West which during 1842 had made comparatively large purchases at the Philadelphia wholesale center.[14]

The report of the Association in October, 1843, indicated a market twice as great as formerly, while their manufactured goods had improved in quality. Part of the recent difficulties had been due to the depression of 1842, when cotton prices had declined sharply. Just then the Association had on hand cotton and cotton goods which had been bought and made at the higher prices which preceded the crash; hence to meet competitive prices they were forced to take a loss on these goods. They had also found that they could not send goods out to be sold by retail dealers on commission, consignment, or credit, since it tied up their small capital. Hence business had to be on a cash basis. This policy was followed by all later wholesalers of free produce goods. In referring to the many troubles which beset them, the committee on manufactures

[11] *Free Labor Advocate*, I, 8 (Feb. 8, 1841).
[12] James Miller McKim (1810-1874) was born at Carlisle, Pa., educated at Dickinson College and Princeton and Andover theological seminaries, and ordained a minister in the Presbyterian church. His advocacy, after 1833, of immediate emancipation antagonized his congregation, whereupon he left the church and devoted the rest of his life to the abolition crusade and to the Negro. He was editor of the *Pennsylvania Freeman*, he protected fugitive slaves, and after 1862 he was very active in the Freedmen's Aid Association.
[13] *Free Labor Advocate*, Sept. 24, 1842.
[14] *Ibid.*, I, 369 (Jan. 27, 1842, May 6, June 24, Aug. 1, 1843). Two such stores were kept by Joel Parker at Newport, and Seth Hinshaw at Greensboro, Ind. The latter advertised that he had "on hand Laguira and St. Domingo coffee, Sandwich Island molasses, Laguira sugar, Manilla and Bengal Indigo. . . ." (*Ibid.*, Nov. 1, 1943.)

mentioned the inferior quality of cotton, its price higher than slave-grown cotton, limited capital which necessitated the manufacture of small lots at heavier costs, and the continued drop in the cotton market generally. They felt, however, that a turn for the better would soon take place, when the price situation would be reversed. During 1843 they had purchased over 30,000 pounds of cotton, and their sales of goods had exceeded $7,000. They had manufactured over 40,000 yards of cloth, which included muslin, shirting, sheeting, printing cloth, bedticking, canton flannel, drilling, Manchester gingham, table diaper, calico, and millinet. During 1844 the outlook continued encouraging. The Association manufactured over 41,000 yards of cloth at a total expense of $8,859.75. Their gross income for the year was $7,805.95.[15] This organization existed for several more years, but no other manufacturing reports are available.

While the Association had its many difficulties in providing goods, the purchasers had their complaints too, as they were voiced by Levi Coffin:

... we have many difficulties to contend with, a lack of confidence in Daniel L Miller, Charles Wise & the great difference in the price of goods and the poorness of the assortment stile &c, are great barriers in the way. The people cannot understand why there should be so much difference in the cost, they believe of course there is an imposition practiced. I have succeeded well in selling Free goods this season notwithstanding these difficulties, but at almost no profit. ... If Free goods can be brought down about on a level with other goods a great many may be sold in the west.[16]

Once more it was time for a renewal of effort in the cause. This came in 1845 with the formation of the Free Produce Association of Friends of Philadelphia Yearly Meeting. The constitution declared that

The Association shall aim to procure correct information of the conditions of the countries with which we have commercial intercourse in respect to free and slave labour, and the means of discriminating between their productions. ... It shall adopt means for obtaining a supply of such articles, the productions of free labour,

[15] American Free Produce Association, *Fifth Annual Report* (1843), pp. 1-11; *Free Labor Advocate*, Jan. 5, 1844, May 10, 1845.
[16] Levi Coffin to Samuel Rhoads, New Garden, Ind., July 18, 1845 (G. W. Taylor MSS).

as are not readily to be procured by individuals through the ordinary channels of commerce or manufacture.[17]

To implement these provisions the Board of Managers, at its first meeting on September 20, 1845, appointed Abraham L. Pennock and Samuel Rhoads to assemble such information.[18]

Rather fortuitously these men had ready to hand enough information to provide an initial report. It came from a letter written the previous spring by Levi Coffin, in which he expressed great confidence (based on his own investigations) that an ample supply of free labor cotton could be obtained in the South. After mentioning the North Carolina supply, he went on to explain how his neighbor, Nathan Thomas, had in 1844 visited relatives in northern Mississippi where he found such cotton available in various places. Coffin had also located some in North Alabama and West Tennessee.[19] Pursuing their inquiries, the committee found other friends of the cause who offered to buy cotton for them, while an English Quaker assured them that "Egyptian cotton may more justly be regarded as *free* produce than otherwise."[20]

Before the next meeting of the Board, another letter had come from Levi Coffin, explaining that Nathan Thomas and his cousin, Moorman Way, had already started to Mississippi on another visit

[17] *Non-Slaveholder*, I, 10 (Jan., 1846).
[18] Philadelphia Free Produce Association, Minutes of the Board of Managers, Sept. 20, 1845, p. 2. Samuel Rhoads (1807-1868) was one of the most active leaders of the Philadelphia Free Produce Association. He was the author of several tracts on slavery, he was editor of the *Non-Slaveholder* from 1846 to 1850, and in 1856 he became editor of the *Friends' Review*, in which capacity he served until a few months before his death.
[19] Levi Coffin to Abraham L. Pennock, April 1, 1845 (G. W. Taylor MSS) (this is a contemporary copy of the original letter); Philadelphia Free Produce Association, Minutes of the Board of Managers, Sept. 27, 1845, p. 7.
[20] Philadelphia Free Produce Association, Minutes of the Board of Managers, Nov. 1, 1846, pp. 21 f. Prior to this meeting the Board of Managers had adopted bylaws and set up standing committees. These were:
Committee on Finance "who shall provide ways and means and certify all bills before they are presented to the Board." Samuel Allinson, Jr., George W. Taylor, and Thomas Wistar, Jr. Committee on Supplies, "to ascertain where Free Produce is to be obtained, and to take measures under the direction of the Board for procuring such articles as may be wanted." Abraham L. Pennock, Israel H. Johnson, Samuel Rhoads, and Samuel Alsop.
Committee on Manufactures, "to superintend the manufacturing of the Products." Samuel Rhoads, Elihu Pickering, Edward Garrett, and Abraham L. Pennock.

to relatives as well as a survey of the free labor cotton situation. Coffin urged the Board to act quickly if they expected to obtain any of that year's crop. Upon the basis of this information the Board, on November 15, 1845, authorized the purchase of fifty bales of cotton.[21]

Being inexperienced in such an undertaking, the committee were somewhat confused as to procedure, but Nathan Thomas, writing from Holly Springs, Mississippi, set them right on several points. He assured them that cash on the spot was necessary and that they could not expect to have cotton shipped without paying for it first. He explained that the small farmers who had free labor cotton for sale needed their money—and could readily sell in the ordinary market. He had engaged about fifty bales for the Association, but would need a bank draft on Memphis as soon as possible. Prices averaged seven cents in the Memphis market, and he was paying no more, but he personally looked after the ginning, and had to pay extra to insure free labor work.[22]

The committee's inquiries addressed to John H. Krafft, a Memphis cotton factor, elicited a very encouraging reply. He claimed that about one fifth of all cotton coming onto the Memphis market was raised by free labor; hence he could furnish a large amount. He added: ". . . they may rely upon my *honour* that every bale shall be strictly 'free labour,' and that each Invoice shall be sworn to before a magistrate and the name and residence of each grower be given."[23] Nathan Thomas ultimately obtained sixty-three bales,

[21] Philadelphia Free Produce Association, Minutes of the Board of Managers, Nov. 15, 1845, p. 22; Levi Coffin to Samuel Rhoads, Newport, Ind., Oct. 30, 1845 (G. W. Taylor MSS).

[22] Nathan Thomas to Samuel Rhoads, Holly Springs, Miss., Nov. 20, 1845 (G. W. Taylor MSS). Thomas's activities were confined chiefly to North Mississippi. His account of the difficulties with ginning is as follows: "[There was] a small additional expence for bailing, in order to make it entirely clear from Slave labour. . . . A part we got white men to handle entirely by renting gins an other part was gined through the Christmas Holladays when the slaves got the entire proffit and the rest we have had to pay the slaves (with the concent of their claimants) for ther survises over and above the usual toll for gining according to the number of them engaged in it as the gins are all owned by the large planters, we have had to seek the most favourable opportunities for having it put up right, which makes by far the greatest difficulty in obtaining free cotton. . . ." Nathan Thomas had a vigorous and alert mind and much practical business sense, but a limited formal education.

[23] J. H. Krafft to Messrs. Brown & Bowen, Dec. 6, 1845 (G. W. Taylor MSS); Philadelphia Free Produce Association, Minutes of the Board of Managers, Feb. 7, 1846, p. 32.

which were shipped by John H. Krafft, and reached Philadelphia in April, 1846. Ten bales of this cotton were sold to Daniel L. Miller, Jr., for the American Free Produce Association.[24]

The difficulties in getting cotton ginned led Nathan Thomas to undertake a better arrangement. The essential need was for gins owned by nonslaveholding farmers. Toward this end Thomas "ventured to order a gin put up in Lafayette County near the had [sic] of navigation to the Talahatchey river" where he thought there could "bee 100 or 150 bails collected . . ." which would mean a supply of cotton at market prices. The Managers concluded to advance as much as three hundred dollars to purchase the gin, which was to be repaid in cotton.[25] John H. Krafft explained the best mode of procedure and assured them that if 1,500 to 2,000 bales could be taken, the cotton would be no higher than slave-grown, but if a small quantity only was handled it would of course cost more. Krafft offered to supervise the whole undertaking if someone to inspect the gins were provided. Krafft was sincerely interested, but he overestimated the financial resources of the free produce associations.[26] On further reflection, he advised against the establishment of gins, for, he said, the cotton Nathan Thomas had bought cost nearly one cent per pound more than it was worth. This was due to the fact that it was bought in rural areas where each farmer thought his crop was worth the top price. If the purchases had been made in a large market with expert evaluation, Krafft was confident the Association would have saved money. He felt sure that several hundred bales of *"pure* free labour cotton" could be had each season in the Memphis market, and if the Association would waive the free labor ginning requirement, many thousand bales would be available. He was willing to enter into such business arrangements as would be mutually advantageous.[27] Krafft continued to be the Association's purchasing agent until his death in August, 1857, and was succeeded by Thomas Leech and Company.

[24] Philadelphia Free Produce Association, Minutes of the Board of Managers, Feb. 2, March 7, April 4, 1846, pp. 33-35; Nathan Thomas to Samuel Rhoads, Memphis, Tenn., Jan. 14, Feb. 13, 1846 (G. W. Taylor MSS).

[25] Philadelphia Free Produce Association, Minutes of the Board of Managers, June 6, 1846, pp. 47 f.; Nathan Thomas to Samuel Rhoads, Jan. 14, 1846 (G. W. Taylor MSS).

[26] J. H. Krafft to Samuel Rhoads, Memphis, Tenn., Jan. 20, 1846 (G. W. Taylor MSS).

[27] J. H. Krafft to Samuel Rhoads, Memphis, Tenn., March 16, 1846 (G. W. Taylor MSS).

At about the same time Nathan Thomas reported his views on the matter and detailed the arrangement he had made for the next season. J. A. and R. S. Hunt of Lafayette County, Mississippi, would supply at least one hundred bales. (It was to these men that the Association loaned three hundred dollars to build a gin.) In Marshall County, Mississippi, there was already a gin operated by free labor which would furnish at least fifty bales. In the same county Nathan Thomas's uncle, Pleasant Diggs, would build a gin if a like amount was loaned him, while a neighbor, William Crow, expected to buy a farm having a gin and therewith supply at least sixty bales. William McRay of Oak Ridge in the same county was so sure of obtaining at least two hundred bales that the Association agreed to lend him money to erect a gin. Others offered to build gins on their own responsibility. Thus Nathan Thomas felt sure of obtaining at least four hundred bales.[28]

His final report on his operations for the winter of 1845-46 was made in April, 1846. The sixty-three bales of cotton he had secured came from fifteen farmers, and varied from two to eleven bales per farm. As to compensation for his own services, Nathan Thomas calculated his additional

expencs war nearly payed by the $15.00 that I drew . . . for traviling while engaged in procuring cotton. . . . [He added] I shall be satisfyed with what ever the managers may think fit to bestow, or if the institution should be limited in its resorces let it slip entirely, however needy I may be let not the caus great caus be paralized the least on my account. . . .

In mentioning the way in which his activities were received in the South he said: ". . . we had no violence shown us although the excitement ran very high in some places. We ware threatened with the civil authorities . . . but we endeavoured to act prudently on all occasions. . . ." In some neighborhoods residents were cautioned to guard their Negro quarters, on the assumption that Thomas's real purpose was "to instill mischief in the heads of the negrows." By having their relatives and local acquaintances accompany them, and by making constant and careful explanations of their purposes, Thomas and his cousin usually succeeded in quieting suspicion.[29]

[28] Nathan Thomas to Samuel Rhoads, New Garden, Ind., March 18, 1846 (G. W. Taylor MSS); Philadelphia Free Produce Association, Minutes of the Board of Managers, June 6, 1846, pp. 47 ff.
[29] Nathan Thomas to Samuel Rhoads, New Garden, Ind., April 8, 1846

All these activities the Managers were able to report to the first annual meeting of the Association on April 21, 1846. Since the cotton was not received until early spring, the Committee on Manufactures did not yet have much tangible evidence of their activities. They also encountered their first difficulties in getting small lots of cloth made so that it would not be mixed with that woven from slave labor cotton. Nevertheless, 10,000 yards of sheeting, calicoes, cambrics, apron checks, pant stuff, and bedticking had been contracted for, and a few pieces were already finished.[30] These goods were turned over for selling to Thomas S. Field and Company. A few months later the Managers decided to ship ten bales of their cotton to Manchester for manufacture into finer fabrics than they could readily have made in the United States.[31]

Since the treasurer's records as such are not available, it is impossible to know the Association's exact financial condition. But from notations in the Minutes of the Managers, a sum between $2,400 and $2,700 was spent up to August 1, 1846. Of this amount, about $1,800 went for cotton and freight charges thereon. The annual report of 1847 noted the permanent capital as being slightly more than $4,000, while the merchandise sold or on hand amounted to $5,500 and the cotton in process to $2,200.[32]

During 1846-47 the Association sent no agent to the South, because arrangements to do so were begun too late in the season. Levi Coffin, however, was active in the work. In August, 1846, he had two sixty-saw gins made at Cincinnati, but when they were

---

(G. W. Taylor MSS). In his further comments Nathan Thomas said, "Here let mee state that great ignorance prevails among the common people, perhaps no more than one white man in twenty that reads the publick papers, and the little and imperfect news on the moovements of the people of the north on the slave question; that reaches them leaves them much in the dark.

"The few that do understand what is going on, deal it out as suits them best, . . . when the poor of that country properly understands the principles of A. S. men they then view them as their best friends, for they feel the Iron heal of aristocracy grinding them down to a level with the slave."

[30] Philadelphia Free Produce Association, Minutes of the Board of Managers, April 17, 1846, pp. 36 f.; *Non-Slaveholder*, I, 65-68 (May, 1846).

[31] Philadelphia Free Produce Association, Minutes of the Board of Managers, Aug. 1, 1846, p. 53.

[32] *Non-Slaveholder*, II, 97 (May, 1847); Philadelphia Free Produce Association, Minutes of the Board of Managers, Feb. 2, April 4, June 6, 1846, pp. 32, 35, 46 f. In May, 1846, Gerrit Smith donated an unspecified amount of money to the Association and indicated his willingness to help "from time to time." Gerrit Smith to Abraham L. Pennock, Peterboro [, N. Y.], May 18, 1846 (*Non-Slaveholder*, I, 94, June, 1846).

ready he found that William McRay could not then take his. The other was sent to the Hunt family. McRay, however, assured Coffin that his cotton crop was very fine, that he would act as agent, that he believed at least 150 bales of free labor cotton could be had in his neighborhood, and that he would rent a gin which would be operated by free labor only. Coffin was also assured of free labor cotton in Yalobusha County, Mississippi, by one Dr. Thacker who lived there. Coffin described him as "a true hearted abolitionist, tho a slave owner at this time," who had tried to settle his slaves in a free state, but met with no encouragement. Coffin continued: ". . . he pays his slaves for their Labor gives them a part of the cotton they raise, he has a Cotton Gin, will raise about 20 bales . . . there can be, he thinks about 150 bales of Free Cotton got in the neighborhood. . . ."[33]

Meanwhile the Managers were trying to arrange for putting large amounts of free labor cotton on the Philadelphia market. Various manufacturers expressed a preference for such cotton, but were unwilling to purchase it themselves or even take it without seeing it first. Hence the Managers had to confine themselves to 200 bales, and they were furthermore very anxious to reduce freight charges and other expenses which had been very high the first year.[34] On account of the high price, the Managers were reluctant to purchase much cotton, but they finally authorized J. H. Krafft to buy "free cotton of good qualities to the amount of about two thousand Dollars." Early in December, 1846, Krafft purchased twenty-four bales at a cost of $1,157.50. Some weeks later the Managers ordered twenty bales "of the *very best* free labour cotton," which was to be shipped to Liverpool for British Friends interested in the cause.[35]

During this year the manufacturing committee encountered much the same difficulties as previously, but succeeded in adding somewhat to the variety of goods and increased the quantity to about 40,000 yards, as well as putting in stock handkerchiefs, hosiery, knitting cotton, and cotton batting.[36] But even when the manufac-

[33] Levi Coffin to Samuel Rhoads, Cincinnati, Aug. 9, 1846 (G. W. Taylor MSS).

[34] Samuel Rhoads to John H. Krafft, Blockly, Pa., Oct. 13, 1846 [draft] (G. W. Taylor MSS).

[35] Samuel Rhoads to J. H. Krafft, Nov. 27, 1846 [draft], Feb. 15, 1847, J. H. Krafft to Samuel Rhoads, Feb. 16, March 19, 1847 (G. W. Taylor MSS).

[36] "To the Board of Managers of Free Produce Association of Friends

turing committee had done its best, the results were not satisfactory to all, as is witnessed by the complaints of an Ohio retailer:

We are [he wrote] very desirous to supply the market here with free Labor goods, and live by it. . . . But unless we can have a better supply of goods and *better* goods than we have been able to get for the last year . . . it will be *impossible to live by the business here!* . . . this year so fare we can get no prints that we can sell at all. . . . We have customers who are wiling to sustain us at a Reasonable sacrifice. But this class is intirely inadequate to sustain us. . . . We would like to know the reason why our Free Labor calicoes are coarser less durable and more faidy than other prints which are manufactured in the Eastern States.[37]

In May, 1847, the Association received a donation of five hundred dollars from Joseph Sturge. This enabled them to plan to send an agent to obtain cotton in the South. Nathan Thomas was again employed.[38] He did not reach Memphis until the middle of December, 1847, but as the price of cotton had fallen since the opening of the season, his delay was considered advantageous. The Hunts, to whom the gin had been supplied, were now "ready to settle the whole debt in Free cotton," since they expected to have at least fifty bales. While Nathan Thomas was procuring cotton for that season, his chief mission, however, was to locate large amounts of free labor cotton, for the Philadelphia association was still optimistic about supplying several mills with free labor cotton exclusively. He reported a large potential amount in the vicinity of Byhalia, Marshall County, Mississippi. Proceeding from there to western Tennessee, he arranged to procure for the next year over seven hundred bales. Thomas also sought to provide rope and bagging of free labor materials.[39]

After many delays in the mails Nathan Thomas received authori-

---

of Philadelphia Yearly Meeting. The Committee on Manufactures Report," April 16, 1847 (G. W. Taylor MSS).

[37] W. R. Wheeler to George W. Taylor, West Elkton, Preble County, Ohio, May 28, 1847 (G. W. Taylor MSS).

[38] Philadelphia Free Produce Association, Minutes of the Board of Managers, May 17, 1847, p. 62; Nathan Thomas to Samuel Rhoads, New Garden, Ind., Jan. 16, 1847 (G. W. Taylor MSS).

[39] Nathan Thomas to G. W. Taylor [actually sent, however, to Samuel Rhoads], Coffeeville [, Miss.], Dec. 20, 1847; Nathan Thomas to Samuel Rhoads, Yalobusha [, Miss.], Dec. 31, 1847; *idem* to *idem*, Lafayette Co., Miss., Jan. 6, 1848; *idem* to *idem*, Marshall Co., Miss., Jan. 11, 1848; *idem* to G. W. Taylor, Jacinto, Miss., Feb. 2, 1848 (G. W. Taylor MSS).

zation to proceed with his journey to Louisiana and Texas, chiefly to find supplies of cotton and rice. In New Orleans he made numerous acquaintances who promised their help, one of whom, John Small, a native of Philadelphia there for his health, agreed to accompany Thomas to Texas. They reached that state early in March, 1848, and during the following weeks made an extensive journey on horseback through eastern Texas and into Arkansas, returning by boat from Little Rock to Memphis. In his report Thomas gave an extensive description of Texas and expressed much hope of the region as a source of free labor products. He had to admit that for the present the cause could expect nothing. The region was too new, settlements too scattered, transportation too little developed, and capital too scarce. As yet most settlers were raising cattle, or food products to sell to newcomers. In Arkansas they found a little cotton. Cotton, sugar, and rice—at least that raised by free labor—were as yet only contemplated. Texas remained for the next decade the great region of hope for the advocates of the free labor cause.[40]

Though unsuccessful in locating free labor sugar or rice, Nathan Thomas made arrangements for procuring over two thousand bales of cotton for the next year. At the same time John H. Krafft of Memphis continued to ship all cotton that the Philadelphia Association purchased. He again deplored the unnecessary expense involved in Thomas's local purchasing. But the latter's procedure was apparently approved by the Managers, for it was part of their purpose to seek out the struggling farmer with the hope of spurring him to greater efforts by the assurance of a great new market where the products of his own labor would actively promote the abolition of an economic system where he must compete with slave labor. Thomas found that his activities created less excitement than had been the case on his previous journey. During the season of 1847-48 J. H. Krafft shipped to Philadelphia on his own account thirty bales of free labor cotton. The Association then ordered thirty to

[40] Nathan Thomas to G. W. Taylor, Grimes Co., Texas, March 12, 1848; *idem* to *idem*, Lavara, Texas, March 24, 1848; *idem* to *idem*, Steamer *E. W. Stephens*, April 16, 1848; *idem* to *idem* [, New Garden, Ind.], May 14, 1848; Nathan Thomas, "[Report] to the Board of Managers of the Friends F. L. Association in Philadelphia," New Garden [, Ind.], April 27, 1848 (G. W. Taylor MSS). Nathan Thomas was paid $300 to cover his expenses and remuneration from the $500 contributed by Joseph Sturge (Philadelphia Free Produce Association, Minutes of the Board of Managers, June 19, 1848, p. 79).

thirty-five bales "of cotton raised and ginned by free labour exclusively to the value of Fifteen hundred dollars."[41]

Meanwhile, from cotton already on hand, the Managers in their annual report (April, 1848) could point to a total of nearly 70,000 yards of cloth manufactured during the preceding year. This represented a considerable increase in varieties and improvement in quality, but they had to confess that prices were still well above the market, since it was necessary to have the weaving done in small mills where the savings of mass production did not operate. They urged adherents of the cause to be patient and promised better results for the future.[42]

In October, 1848, a fundamental change in operations took place when the stock of goods belonging to the Association was transferred to George W. Taylor, at a total valuation of $5,993.80. Also placed at his disposal were the "permanent fund loaned without interest" amounting to $4,500 and outright donations totaling $440. At the same time Robert Lindley Murray, proprietor of the New York store, was guaranteed against loss to the extent of five hundred dollars in his enterprise to buy free labor cotton and send it to the Liverpool market. Under this arrangement Murray shipped about two hundred bales. In the search for other free labor products the Association undertook to ascertain "the present condition of the emancipated population of the British West Indies. . . ."[43]

In 1849 Nathan Thomas once more prepared to journey through the South in search of cotton. This time he was accompanied by Henry Charles, a young Quaker who "has been a warm friend to the slave for many years, and an abstainer from the proceeds as far as practicable." They reached Memphis at the end of November, 1849, and devoted themselves mostly to seeking out gins operated by free labor, inquiring from neighborhood to neighborhood. About this time the "cottage gin" came to the attention of the Managers. This was a small-sized, cheaply priced cotton gin manufactured in England for use in British India. The Managers soon ordered one

[41] Philadelphia Free Produce Association, Minutes of the Board of Managers, Jan. 17, 1848; John H. Krafft to Samuel Rhoads, Memphis, Tenn., Jan. 17, 1848 (G. W. Taylor MSS).
[42] Philadelphia Free Produce Association, Minutes of the Board of Managers, Report of the Manufacturing Committee, March 10, 1848, p. 75.
[43] Philadelphia Free Produce Association, Minutes of the Board of Managers, Oct. 9, Nov. 13, 1848, pp. 81 f.; *Non-Slaveholder*, IV, 97 ff. (May, 1849); *Friend* (London), VII, 76 (April, 1849).

and later shipped it to Cincinnati, where Levi Coffin arranged to have several made if the sample should prove satisfactory.[44] Nathan Thomas immediately asked that one be sent to William McRay. He found that Anderson Hunt, to whom the first gin had been sent in 1847, had so far fallen into error as to hire a slave, but, Thomas added, "I was gratified in learning that they did not put off their cotton as F. L. Cotton. . . ."[45]

Nathan Thomas's itinerary this season was somewhat different. While he and Henry Charles spent some time in northern Mississippi and West Tennessee, they also traveled extensively through North Alabama.[46] From there they went to Mobile and thence to New Orleans "to investigate more fully the shugar business."[47] Late in January, 1850, they were back in North Alabama, and expected to go from there to Georgia. The frustration of this plan Nathan Thomas described thus:

And now dear friend I come to a *waty* matter with us, that is, under the present exited state of public sentiment a doubt of the propriety of extending our mission through Georgia and what makes it more trying to us is not having an opportunity of confering with you on the matter; It appears to be the expectation of all the reading portion of community that a *desalootion* is about *certain* and arraingments are already making by some for such an *event;* true the most of the F. community are not advised on this matter only

[44] Nathan Thomas to Samuel Rhoads, New Garden, Ind., March 22, 1849 (G. W. Taylor MSS); *Non-Slaveholder*, IV, 97 ff. (May, 1849).

[45] Nathan Thomas to Samuel Rhoads, Holly Springs, Miss., Dec. 3, 8, 1849 (G. W. Taylor MSS).

[46] Nathan Thomas to Samuel Rhoads, Carrollton, Ala., Dec. 20, 1849; Franklin Co., Ala., Jan. 22, 1850 (G. W. Taylor MSS).

[47] Nathan Thomas to Samuel Rhoads, New Orleans, Jan. 2, 1850 (G. W. Taylor MSS). In his report to the Board of Managers, Thomas explained this effort: "The object of our going to New Orleans was to find F. L. Shugar and Rice and after we wrote we went in Company with Friend Fuller to the Shugar Levee and inquired of those men that ware the most acquainted in the shugar country, but could find or hear of non Woodland who had the Germans at work on a shuga farm, as reported in my last had abandoned the project sold out to a slave holder. The great expence of erecting a shugar mill prevents poor people from engaging in it when those large mills with steam engines are erected. they superseed the old plan of grinding by horse power; so far that the latter plan appears to be entirely abandoned. The poor people that live in the shugar country raise cotton insted of shugar, and from what we could hear it appeared useless for us to go up the cost [i.e. coast] to enquire further" (Nathan Thomas "[Report] to Board of Managers of Free Produce Association of Friends of Philadelphia Yearly Meeting," New Garden, Ind., Feb. 14, 1850, G. W. Taylor MSS).

by the planters and then in a way suited to arous them in an unproffitable manner. the tide of publick sentiment is evidently getting more and more prejudised against the North. further the feelings of S. Carolina and Georgia is such that I doubt our getting an agent to attend to it at Charleston or Savanna if we ware to find cotton in Geo. . . .

It is only from a wish to do for the *best*, that we think of declining going much further in the work, true it is a heart rending business. . . .[48]

They left Alabama shortly thereafter and reached home on February 6, 1850. Their report detailed more fully the difficulties just alluded to. They found that they were watched almost constantly and that all kinds of rumors were spread as to the nature of their business. Many who were personally willing to assist them found it unwise to do so. When they were in Autauga County, Alabama, for the second time the planter (R. Morton) with whom they were staying would not permit them to call at the post office for their mail. He sent a local boy who, however, was not given the mail there for them. It was only through Morton's stern insistence that they received two personal letters. In many places they found it advisable to depart as soon as their business was concluded and before their presence had aroused much suspicion.[49]

Besides presenting a written report, Nathan Thomas went to Philadelphia for the annual meeting of the Free Produce Association, where he spoke to the assemblage and conferred with the Eastern leaders. He went home by way of New York, where he saw Benjamin Tatham, Secretary of the New York Free Produce Association. In Rochester he visited Frederick Douglass.[50] This was Nathan Thomas's last outstanding work for the cause. He endeavored to promote the sale of Taylor's free labor goods to various retail dealers in Indiana, and occasionally he lectured a little. Nathan Thomas died on August 22, 1851, of cholera, leaving his affairs in a badly confused state. It appears that he had joined Nathan Stanton

[48] Nathan Thomas to Samuel Rhoads, Franklin Co., Ala., Jan. 22, 1850 (G. W. Taylor MSS).

[49] Nathan Thomas, "[Report] to Board of Managers of Free Produce Association of Friends of Philadelphia Yearly Meeting," Feb. 14, 1850, New Garden, Ind. (G. W. Taylor MSS).

[50] Nathan Thomas to Samuel Rhoads, New Garden, Ind., March 13, 20, May 7, 1850 (G. W. Taylor MSS). Thomas's trip to Philadelphia interfered seriously with his farming operations. Frederick Douglass strongly endorsed the free produce cause.

in operating a free labor store and died owing George W. Taylor $1,134.46.[51]

Year by year the search for cotton went on. As Nathan Thomas's work had fully shown, there was an ample supply of free labor cotton within the United States. The difficulty came in segregating it. Because of this the friends of free labor were constantly alert to find supplies of cotton in other parts of the world. This proved to be chiefly a matter of "great expectations," but during the decade of the 1850's some real progress was made. Within this country Texas continued to be the great hope. As early as 1855 German immigrants there raised six hundred bales.[52] Various parts of Africa were looked upon as great potential cotton-growing regions. One of these was Algeria, where the French were reportedly encouraging its cultivation. Optimists predicted that "we shall soon have the finest fabrics of French manufacture from free labor cotton."[53] Central Africa, where, as a missionary reported, "*Cotton* grows *spontaneously*," also aroused great anticipations. During 1857 some 1,250 bales of 100 pounds each had actually been imported "by Thomas Clegg, a large cotton spinner of Manchester." In 1859 some 4,000 pounds of African cotton arrived in Boston, while in Liberia the situation was reported to be promising.[54] South America and Australia were also looked upon as sources of supply, together with the West Indies, British India, and other parts of the Far East.[55] An experiment at Port Natal, South Africa, did not succeed. Furthermore, no sea island cotton produced by free labor was ever found.[56]

This anxious quest for cotton in distant regions had behind it the hope that if a sufficient amount could be had from such areas it

[51] G. W. Taylor to Nathan Stanton, Aug. 23, 1852 (Taylor Letterbooks, I, 22 f.); *Friends' Review*, IV, 825 (Sept. 13, 1851). This obituary notice does not give Thomas's age, but mentions that his father, Benjamin Thomas, died on the same day of the same disease.

[52] *Friends' Review*, IX, 90 (Oct. 20, 1855).

[53] *Vergennes* (Vt.) *Citizen*, Aug. 6, 1856; *Friends' Review*, IX, 53-56 (Oct. 6, 1855).

[54] *Vergennes Citizen*, Jan. 2, 1857; *Friends' Review*, XI, 558 (May 8, 1858); XII, 792 (Aug. 20, 1859); XIII, 343 (Feb. 4, 1860).

[55] Free Produce Association of Friends of New York Yearly Meeting, *Minutes of the Board of Managers* (1853), p. 3; *Burritt's Citizen of the World*, II, 93 (June, 1856). G. W. Taylor was ready to buy some of this African cotton until he found that the fibers were too short for spinning, and so revoked his order.

[56] G. W. Taylor to Elihu Burritt, July 18, 1853 (Taylor Letterbooks, I, 252).

would ultimately offer serious competition to United States cotton. When that time arrived Great Britain would turn to cotton produced in her own colonies and might even levy a protective duty which would ruin the market for American cotton. Then the South would emancipate its slaves whose labor would no longer bring in profits. Even without tariffs, advocates of the cause were sure that such a condition would prove the superiority and economy of free labor.[57]

Passing reference has been made to products other than cotton. It now remains to give a little more attention to them. Prior to the abolition of slavery in the British colonies, sugar produced by free labor was one of the most difficult articles to obtain. The chief trouble was that slave-grown West Indian sugar was protected by the laying of a heavy duty on sugar produced in British India and other parts of the Far East.[58] This made the price prohibitive. Mexico was another source optimistically looked to, largely because of a report on the subject by Sir Henry G. Ward, British envoy to Mexico.[59] The search for all products was accompanied by much wishful thinking, or at least unjustified optimism. In 1828 an article appeared claiming that sugar could easily be raised as far north as latitude 33°, and that the raising of the crop was simple, easy, healthful, and did not require much capital. Benjamin Lundy seized on this as a happy augury of what might be expected in the future.[60] Meanwhile, Lundy's report to the American Convention in 1828 gave definite assurance that sugar was produced by free labor in at least two islands of the West Indies. Again he became hopeful in announcing that a company had purchased land in Florida for the purpose of raising sugar.[61] An even more fantastic scheme came

---

[57] The condition of free labor in these areas was scarcely ever alluded to. Advocates of the free labor cause had their eyes intently fixed on whether labor was legally slave or legally free. The fact that colonial "free" labor was consistently exploited so that the condition of the individual might be no better than if he were a slave, was ignored at this time. Allusion to it was very rare, as was also any reference to exploitation of cotton mill workers either in Britain or the United States.

[58] *Genius of Universal Emancipation*, IV, 172 (Aug., 1825); VII, 70, 123 (Sept. 2, Oct. 20, 1827).

[59] *Ibid.*, X, 105 (Dec. 11, 1829). Ward's report was dated March 13, 1826, and was taken by Lundy from the *Anti-Slavery Monthly Reporter* for Aug., 1829. Ward had personally investigated sugar growing by free labor in various parts of Mexico. His favorable report was widely noticed by anti-slavery leaders.

[60] *Genius of Universal Emancipation*, VIII, 70 (March 15, 1828).

[61] American Convention . . . , *Minutes* (Adjourned Session, 1828), pp. 25 ff.

to light in 1832, when a resident of Jaffrey, New Hampshire, built a plant for making sugar and molasses from potatoes, while in 1841 an effort to make sugar from corn was announced.[62]

One kind of free labor sugar always available was maple sugar, which was regularly stocked by all free labor stores. This, combined with such other as could be obtained, provided a reasonably adequate supply. During 1829 Charles Pierce's free labor store in Philadelphia reported the purchase of over $4,000 worth of free labor sugar and molasses.[63] Some of this he obtained from Puerto Rico, of a Spanish planter who did not have slaves, but used free labor. At about this time "*White* India Sugar" was advertised in New York at 12 1-2 cents per pound. In 1839 a Boston merchant advertised "FREE LABOR MOLASSES from the Sandwich Islands."[64]

In their address to the New York Free Produce Association, the Board of Managers of the Philadelphia association enumerated Mexico, LaGuayra, and Manila as sources for sugar; and Java, Santo Domingo, LaGuayra, and Maracaibo as coffee-producing areas.[65] In 1847 the Philadelphia association became concerned over the sale of Puerto Rican sugar and molasses as free labor products, and asked the New York association to make special investigations so that no fraud should be practiced. They felt that the British West Indies and various South American countries were more reliable sources. Often they had to take advantage of a chance supply as happened when the Boston Sugar Refinery informed Taylor that it had purchased several cargoes of Manila sugar which would go through the refinery in about two weeks and would sell as "11c for loaf and crushed, and 11 1-2c for powdered—5% off for cash."[66]

On his tour in 1847-48 for cotton, Nathan Thomas heard of

[62] *Liberator*, II, 51 (March 31, 1832); *Pennsylvania Freeman*, Sept. 29, 1841.
[63] *Genius of Universal Emancipation*, X, 58 (Oct. 30, 1829).
[64] *Ibid.*; *SUGAR from another HEMISPHERE*, advertised by N. Very [n.p., n.d., *ca.* Nov. 24, 1830? a broadside]; *Liberator*, IX, 43 (March 15, 1839). This molasses probably came from Koloa Plantation, the first sugar plantation in the Hawaiian Islands (Arthur C. Alexander, *Koloa Plantation, 1835-1935: A History of the Oldest Hawaiian Sugar Plantation*, Honolulu, 1937, pp. 1-24).
[65] Philadelphia Free Produce Association, Minutes of the Board of Managers, Oct. 4, 1845, p. 10.
[66] *Ibid.*, May 17, 1847, p. 10; Rice & Thaxton to G. W. Taylor, Boston, April 28, 1847 (G. W. Taylor MSS).

one Louisiana sugar planter who had hired thirty German immigrants to work one hundred acres of cane. His hopes from this source were dashed, however, when he learned early in 1850 that the planter "had abandoned the project [and] sold out to a slave holder."[67]

In 1850 the question of Puerto Rican sugar still weighed heavily upon the Managers of the Philadelphia association, and so they determined to send George W. Taylor on a trip of personal investigation. Taylor sailed on November 9, 1850. In Bermuda he found the emancipated Negroes "pressed down by so many disabilities that their condition is still far from comfortable." In St. Thomas he devoted himself to inquiries about Puerto Rico and was assured "that there were no estates . . . cultivated wholly without slaves." A letter to a Puerto Rican merchant resulted in further corroboration of this fact. Meanwhile Taylor visited Saint Croix, where he "became persuaded that here was the place for obtaining supplies of sugar and molasses." After investigating the situation to his complete satisfaction Taylor engaged a young Quaker who had accompanied him to visit Barbados, Trinidad, and Demarara, to make further inquiries. By the early spring of 1851 Taylor had obtained a modest supply of Saint Croix sugar and molasses made from the new crop. In 1853 the Managers could tell the Philadelphia association that "the British, French and Danish West Indies, so recently the strongholds of slavery," could now be looked to as sources of free labor sugar.[68]

It was not long before another ephemeral scheme for making sugar caught the attention of free labor adherents. Beginning in 1856, they were confronted with numerous articles on the virtues of "Chinese sugar cane" (sorghum cane). Experiments in various

[67] Nathan Thomas to G. W. Taylor, Harden Co., Tenn., Jan. 25, 1848; Nathan Thomas, "[Report] To Board of Managers of Free Produce Association of Friends of Philadelphia Yearly Meeting," Feb. 14, 1850 (G. W. Taylor MSS).

[68] Philadelphia Free Produce Association, Minutes of the Board of Managers, May 12, 1851, pp. 88 ff.; *Friends' Review*, VI, 635 f. (June 18, 1853). In this connection G. W. Taylor asked Elihu Burritt to make "enquiry for me through thy French, Belgian and Dutch correspondents, in relation to the practicability of my importing from either of those countries, Refined, Loaf, crushed or ground Sugars—The U. S. duty is 30 per cent. ad valorem If I could know the cost & probable freight to Philada. I could make my calculations—I mean *free labour* Sugar—either refined from the Beet root sugar wholly or from a mixture of that & Manilla or English, French or Danish West India sugars—" (G. W. Taylor to Elihu Burritt, Sept. 3, 1852, Taylor Letterbooks, I, 29).

parts of the country soon showed that it would produce satisfactory molasses, while all firmly believed that "our chemists will soon teach us how to convert the syrup into sugar for *export*."[69] The heavy duty on foreign sugar to protect Louisiana planters, and the vast increase in price due to poor crops made the development of sorghum doubly necessary. High prices for cane sugar also led to a great increase in the manufacture of maple sugar. Of this kind, 34,253,436 pounds had been produced in 1850, while it was estimated that in 1857 the amount was almost 70,000,000 pounds. In 1859 Taylor advertised a supply of syrup "made from the AFRICAN IMPHEE" (a variety of sorghum).[70]

The best hopes for a supply of free labor rice appeared when it was found that some nonslaveholding farmers in eastern North Carolina raised a little rice. Steps were immediately taken to purchase what was available, and this, it was hoped, would quickly lead to increased cultivation. To this end Charles Pierce in 1831 and 1832 offered a premium of twenty dollars for five to ten casks of rice. This stimulus probably did not have the desired effect, for in 1833 Joseph H. Beale, who had a wholesale free produce store in New York, imported rice from the East Indies.[71]

Late in 1846 Henry Miles made a journey to Virginia in search of free labor produce. In the counties of Southampton, Nansemond, and Isle of Wight he discovered anew that a few Friends raised small amounts of indigo, cotton, and rice. After seeing several patches of rice he was convinced that assurance of a steady market would bring a good supply at fifty to seventy-five cents a bushel. The next season thirty bushels were secured from Southampton County, while more was expected from Perquimans County, North Carolina.[72] Taylor's inquiries about tropical products in Liberia elicited the reply that as yet that country produced little more than it consumed. A packet line had just been established, and a little coffee had been shipped. Rice could be sent in a rough state, and ginger was available.[73]

[69] *Friends' Review*, X, 184 (Nov. 29, 1856); *Vergennes Citizen*, Sept. 18, 1857. Henry Miles was one of the experimenters.
[70] *Friends' Review*, X, 344, 575 (Feb. 7, May 16, 1857); XIII, 154 (Nov. 12, 1859).
[71] *Genius of Universal Emancipation*, X, 58 (Oct. 30, 1829); XII, 136 (Jan., 1832); XIII, 83 (April, 1833); *Liberator*, I, 93 f. (June 11, 1831).
[72] Henry Miles to Elihu Burritt, Monkton, Vt., Nov. 4, 1846 (Henry Miles MSS, Harvard); *Friends' Review*, I, 547 f. (May 20, 1848).
[73] Stephen "A" Beuron to G. W. Taylor, Bassa Cove [, Liberia], Nov. 1, 1848 (G. W. Taylor MSS).

THE FREE PRODUCE MOVEMENT 81

Finally, the distribution of free labor goods through stores needs a brief summary.[74] The first known store was that of Benjamin Lundy and Michael Lamb, opened at Baltimore in 1826. It lasted about six months. Between that and the close of 1829 at least eight stores were opened in New York, Philadelphia, and New Jersey towns. Of these, only two had any permanence. In New York, Charles Collins had, according to his own statement, operated a free produce store since 1817, and he continued to do so until 1843 or later. James and Charles Pierce in Philadelphia maintained a store for some years. During 1830-31 nine more stores were opened.[75]

Prominent among these stores was that of Lydia White, opened at Philadelphia in May, 1830. A Quaker of the Hicksite branch, she was for years one of the most zealous proponents of free labor. In 1831 she was receiving orders for goods from Vermont, Rhode Island, New York, Ohio, Indiana, Delaware, Pennsylvania, and New Jersey. She was also purchasing on her own initiative small amounts of cotton and having it manufactured. Of her activities she wrote, "I am increasingly desirous to do what I can in this way, to encourage the conscientious in abstinence from the products of the slaves' labor. . . ."[76] From 1838 to 1846 she acted as retail agent for the American Free Produce Association, while J. Miller McKim took care of the wholesale trade. She continued the work until early in 1846, when Joel Fisher bought out her store.

Between 1832 and 1837 only four new stores appeared. Of these, one kept by Joseph H. Beale in New York was advertised as a wholesale establishment.[77] Before 1840 six more stores, three of them in Philadelphia, two in Boston, and one in Lynn, Massachusetts, began operations. That of Charles Wise in Philadelphia continued until 1843.[78] The decade of the 1840's saw the opening of

[74] The Appendix gives a list of all stores which have come to the writer's attention.

[75] Charles Collins (1803-Oct. 12, 1878) declared in 1842 that he had conducted a free produce store for twenty-five years. If these dates are correct, he was only fourteen when he began business (*Friends' Intelligencer*, XXXV, 537, Oct. 12, 1878; *Liberator*, I, 87, May 28, 1831).

[76] *Liberator*, I, 87 (May 28, 1831). This issue quotes a letter from Lydia White to William Lloyd Garrison; *Pennsylvania Freeman*, April 11, 1844.

[77] *Genius of Universal Emancipation*, XIII, 83 (April, 1833); *Liberator*, IV, 103 (June 28, 1834). Beale was in business for at least two years, 1833-Jan., 1835.

[78] Charles Wise's store was in operation at the beginning of 1837 and

many small stores in the West. By 1845 there were five in Indiana.

The latter half of the decade witnessed considerable reorganization for more effective operation. During 1846 Joel Fisher acted as agent for the Philadelphia Free Produce Association. A better arrangement came about in 1847, when George W. Taylor bought him out and made Philadelphia the center of both wholesale and retail trade. Taylor continued in business until 1867. Under the auspices of the New York Free Produce Association, Lindley Murray Hoag and George Wood opened a store at New York in January, 1848. They soon became so discouraged that in September of the same year Robert Lindley Murray took over the work. He continued until February, 1852, when his foreman, Ezra Towne, took charge of the store. Towne carried a stock of free labor groceries and some dry goods until 1860 or later.[79]

In the West the Mount Pleasant Free Labor Company operated a retail store from 1848 to 1863. The only wholesale agency was that of Levi Coffin begun at Cincinnati in 1847 and continued for ten years. There were doubtless many more stores than those here mentioned, and even more general merchants who kept small stocks of free labor goods to meet the demands of their Quaker customers.[80]

---

possibly earlier. Wise (1811-June 29, 1895) belonged to various anti-slavery societies and was active in Underground Railroad work.

[79] Robert Lindley Murray (Nov. 11, 1825-Aug. 29, 1874), the son of Robert I. Murray and Elizabeth (Colden) Murray, was born in New York City. He was educated at Friends' schools and Haverford College. He engaged for a time in the wool trade and later entered the insurance business. Besides his great interest and activity in the free produce cause, he participated in many other philanthropic measures and devoted much time to religious matters. He died as the result of a fall from his carriage (*Friends' Review*, XXVIII, 91, Sept. 26, 1874; *From under His Wings: A Sketch of the Life of Robert Lindley Murray*, New York, 1876, pp. 56, 60 f., 65).

[80] Most of the information concerning stores has necessarily been gathered from their advertisements, which obviously are not entirely a satisfactory source. The nonappearance of a given store's advertisement cannot be taken as proof that the store went out of business. Advertising appeared, furthermore, only in sympathetic journals, and that in newspapers was almost entirely local. If a paper changed its policy, the free produce stores stopped advertising. This was the case in the *Liberator* and to some extent in the *Pennsylvania Freeman*. The chief source of information for the entire West is the *Free Labor Advocate* (1841-48).

CHAPTER V

George W. Taylor and His Work

No one was more faithful in the free produce cause than George W. Taylor. From 1845 onward and especially after 1847 he devoted his whole time, energy, and capital to promotion of the cause. He conducted the free produce store in Philadelphia for twenty years (1847-67) and bore the brunt of all the difficulties in obtaining goods, the complaints of customers, the delays, disappointments, and the financial sacrifices involved. Taylor was a careful businessman with some experience in merchandising before he opened his free produce store. It was due to his careful attention to details and his keen business judgment that the enterprise was kept going at all.

George Washington Taylor (March 14, 1803-January 10, 1891) was born in Radnor, Pennsylvania, the son of Jacob Taylor (1772-1866) and Elizabeth Richards Taylor (1776-1868). His mother was the daughter of David and Elizabeth (Megee) Richards, of Welsh descent, and of strong Quaker antecedents. Taylor's paternal grandfather was Francis Taylor, born at Staines near London, the son of Richard and Mary Taylor. Francis Taylor came to America before the Revolution, married Eve Fisler, a Dutch woman, and settled in Chester County, Pennsylvania, where their ten children were born.

George W. Taylor was the oldest of Jacob and Elizabeth Taylor's seven children. His father kept a country store at Kaolin, Chester County, in which George assisted when he became old enough. He grew up in a strongly religious atmosphere, although neither parent was a communicant of any church until 1815, when George and his mother became members of the Society of Friends at New Garden, Pennsylvania, as did all his brothers and sisters in later years. His father attended meetings but never became a member.

Taylor's mother made special exertions to see that her children were educated. George as a small boy was a diligent student and usually led his class. The local teachers were soon not qualified to give him further instruction, whereupon he entered Enoch Lewis's school, which was nearby. Enoch Lewis, one of the most distinguished Quaker teachers of his day, was an expert mathematician. After two quarters under Lewis, George Taylor taught school, earning enough to attend Enoch Lewis's classes for eight months together where he "completed a full and thorough course in mathematics and was qualified to teach all its branches."

During his youth Taylor exhibited a strongly religious turn of mind. Soon after becoming a Friend, he adopted Quaker dress and wore "plain coats" the rest of his life. Some years later he felt it his duty "to use the plain language grammatically . . . though it was much in the cross." At about the age of twenty he began to speak in meeting, although he found it a great trial. His temperance and anti-slavery principles developed at about the same time.

After completing his schooling with Enoch Lewis, Taylor began to teach in his home neighborhood. Very shortly, however, he was offered a position in a Friends' boarding school at Flushing, Long Island. He went there about 1827 and remained until 1829, when he resigned and took an extensive trip to western Pennsylvania and Ohio. There he visited numerous aunts, uncles, and cousins.

After teaching another school in rooms above his father's store, Taylor in 1830 accepted a position at Westtown School, near Philadelphia, where he remained for two sessions. On September 15, 1831, he married Elizabeth Sykes, who had also been a teacher there. They removed to her home locality of Burlington, New Jersey, where George took over the Friends' Preparative Meeting School. He continued teaching until the heavy work affected his health, and in 1834 he accepted "the agency of The Friends Bible and Tract Association and the publishing agency of *The Friend*." To these activities Taylor soon added bookbinding. These occupations he pursued with considerable success until he took over the free produce store in 1847, which did not close its doors until 1867.

Meantime Taylor's wife, who was some years older than he, died on December 24, 1859. On October 12, 1864, he married Ruth Leeds, and in 1867 moved to his parents' farm, which he had bought after his father's death. There he carried on farming and dairying. Ruth Leeds Taylor died on April 24, 1881. On May 27, 1885, Taylor married Elizabeth Burton, a woman several years younger than he. She survived his death on January 10, 1891, at the age of eighty-seven.[1]

[1] George Washington Taylor, *Autobiography and Writings of George W.*

Taylor's activities in conducting his free produce business fall into several categories, which will be discussed in turn. After 1849 he was responsible for finding supplies of free labor products, although the Philadelphia association helped him to the extent of financing his trip to the West Indies, and of sending Nathan Thomas to procure cotton. Taylor, however, was personally responsible for getting the cotton manufactured. He endeavored to supply the entire market for free labor cotton cloth, assisted to a limited degree by Levi Coffin, who had a few varieties of coarse cloth manufactured in the West. Free labor groceries were supplied chiefly through the New York store whose proprietor sold wholesale to Taylor. Factors in his retail trade were the limited demand for and supply of goods, the efforts to satisfy customers, and the financial limitations of the business. Taylor also did a mail order business with individuals and small groups of Friends. All this involved a vast amount of correspondence, while the store demanded much detailed work in packing and shipping orders. In the latter Taylor of course had help. Besides, he was Secretary of the Board of Managers of the Philadelphia Free Produce Association, he had other philanthropic interests, and he was always active in a religious capacity, all of which made him a very busy man.

At the beginning of 1853 Taylor purchased his business location on the northwest corner of Fifth and Cherry streets, for $8,500, which he considered a reasonable price. He had twenty feet fronting on Fifth Street and sixty-seven on Cherry. He then erected a four-story building on the portion of the ground not already covered by a building of similar height. The new structure served as his residence while he remained in the free produce business.[2]

From the very outset manufacturing presented difficulties. In 1847 the Manufacturing Committee of the Philadelphia association reported that they found several manufacturers who would agree to use free labor cotton exclusively in their mills, but few who would clear their machinery in order to run through a few bales of cotton. Those who would do so could turn out only a limited variety of

---

Taylor (Philadelphia, 1891), pp. 5, 17, 18, 39, 46, and *passim;* and information furnished by Francis R. Taylor of Philadelphia. George W. Taylor wrote this account of his life in 1887.

[2] G. W. Taylor to Josias F. Browne, Jan. 31, 1853, June 19, 1854 (Taylor Letterbooks, I, 136, 388). The building erected by Taylor is still standing.

goods. Furthermore, the association never had funds enough to buy sufficient cotton to keep several mills at capacity operation. The committee made such arrangements as it could in the face of these handicaps.[3]

Constant inquiries frequently brought to light mills with apparently encouraging possibilities. One such was the mill of Job Eddy at New Bedford, Massachusetts. He used about 300 bales of cotton a year in making common and coarse cloth. In 1849 he was willing to take thirty bales of free labor cotton at 8¼ cents for manufacture into printing cloths at 4¼ cents per yard.[4] Since most mills could not restrict themselves to free labor cotton, Taylor frequently sent his cotton to be run through as a unit, but without clearing the machinery, so that at the beginning and end of the run it was mixed with the slave labor cotton. He then took only that cloth which was unmixed. When one mill refused to take as small an amount as fourteen bales he tried another, explaining how badly he needed fine shirting and sheeting.[5]

Early in 1853 Taylor sought out a manufacturer who had formerly printed calicoes for him and was now in that business again. In making his inquiries as to prices, etc., Taylor remarked that he was not satisfied with much of the printing he had done in this country, while that done in England was too costly.[6] Plainness of dress was one of the strong Quaker testimonies; hence colors and designs in cloth were somewhat limited. The distinctive Quaker colors were drab, brown, and gray, while patterns in calicoes and ginghams must be small, neat, and "quiet." There was no sale for the various shades of blue, to say nothing of reds, greens, yellows, or purples. Taylor had much trouble in getting suitable patterns and colors, especially in the goods made in England.

Manufacture of goods in Britain bulked large in Taylor's affairs for a number of years. As early as 1847 the Philadelphia associa-

[3] Report of the Manufacturing Committee to the Board of Managers of the Philadelphia Free Produce Association, April 16, 1847 (G. W. Taylor MSS).

[4] William C. Taber to G. W. Taylor, New Bedford [, Mass.], Feb. 24, 1849 (G. W. Taylor MSS). Printing cloth was the unfinished material which, when printed, became calico. Taylor usually had the printing done himself in order to obtain colors and designs suited to his customers.

[5] G. W. Taylor to Joseph Bancroft, Sept. 4, 1852; G. W. Taylor to Gideon C. Smith, July 29, 1852 (Taylor Letterbooks, I, 1, 32 f.). Smith's mill was at Pawtucket, R. I.

[6] G. W. Taylor to Isaac P. Wendall, March 8, 1853 (Taylor Letterbooks, I, 170)

tion sent some cotton to Liverpool with a view to having it manufactured in England.[7] How much of this was done prior to 1852 cannot be indicated for want of records. But in that year Taylor was having part of his manufacturing done by Josias F. Browne and Company of Manchester. Browne, a Quaker much interested in the free labor cause, was a leader of the movement in England. He doubtless did the best he could, but the results were often far from what Taylor needed. Terminology in the two countries differed, so that when Taylor would ask for a particular cloth by name, Browne would send something entirely different. Colors and patterns were often unsuitable, and occasionally goods arrived in a damaged condition, as the result of poor packing or imperfect printing. In commenting on such a circumstance Taylor wrote: ". . . the printed linen cambrics . . . appear to be very badly printed . . . so much so that ladies who wanted dresses of them would not take them on that account. . . . My customers are exceedingly particular."[8]

Another difficulty was the impossibility of getting goods when they were needed. Seasonal demands required a good stock of spring and fall goods, to arrive about March and September, respectively. Delays, unavoidable or otherwise, in Browne's shipments often resulted in their arrival months after they were needed. This meant that Taylor would have to hold them over until the next season, a procedure which helped to tie up his limited capital. Somehow, one hundred bales of cotton which R. L. Murray had shipped to Liverpool early in 1852, did not reach those who were to manufacture it; hence this seriously curtailed the supply of goods for the fall trade.[9] In December, 1852, Taylor began to be anxious about his goods for the spring trade. He had been much handicapped up to that time by having no canton flannel for his fall trade. It seemed impossible for him to make Browne & Company understand what that particular cloth was and his urgent need for it. In December he implored Browne to let him know what kinds of cloths were in preparation for spring, and tried to impress upon him the great need for "a

[7] John H. Krafft to Samuel Rhoads, Memphis, Tenn., March 19, 1847 (G. W. Taylor MSS).

[8] G. W. Taylor to Josias F. Browne & Co., Aug. 10, 1852 (Taylor Letterbooks, I, 5). Correspondence over this lot of damaged goods continued for over a year, while Taylor tried to sell the items as best he could (*idem* to *idem*, Nov. 1, 1853).

[9] G. W. Taylor to Ezra Towne, Oct. 16, 1852 (Taylor Letterbooks, I, 54).

supply of pant stuff," while, he added, "the Delains will be out of season I fear altogether."[10]

By the middle of February, 1853, Taylor was assured of a reasonably good supply of staple spring goods from England. Even so, he still looked anxiously for other needed items, and found on the receipt of some that they were badly damaged from inadequate packing. In an effort to supply the deficiencies Taylor sent twelve bales of cotton to Browne with instructions to manufacture it and ship back the goods as soon as they were ready. But the delay seriously handicapped him, and so Taylor warned Josias Browne that he could not advance money for purchasing cotton, hence some other arrangement must be made.[11] For his fall trade Taylor received a shipment of goods from John Wingrave, a manufacturer of Carlisle, England. But this was quite insufficient in amount and variety. At the first of October, 1853, Taylor was still looking in vain for fall goods from Josias Browne and then wrote in desperation to know what had become of the goods which were to have been made from cotton he had shipped the preceding February. When a shipment did arrive some days later, Taylor was still impelled to write: "I have suffered heavily in my small business and the cause has been much dampened by the non arrival of Prints medium shirtings, sheetings, Canton flannel, drillings, coloured sewing cotton, hosiery and a variety of articles much wanted besides."[12]

Early in 1854 Taylor shipped fifteen bales of free labor cotton to John Wingrave, part of which he wanted made up into 3,000 yards of "grandrills or heavy twilled stuff (of cotton) for pantaloons for working men and boys." Throughout the spring and summer Taylor continued to urge Browne to send goods and send them quickly. The expense of shipping the cotton to England, plus

[10] G. W. Taylor to Josias F. Browne & Co., Dec. 14, 1852, Jan. 11, 1853 (Taylor Letterbooks, I, 106). Canton flannel, a heavy cotton material, twilled on one side and with a nap on the other, was widely used for underclothing, especially in the West. Heavy cotton cloth for making men's work trousers was an indispensable item for the spring trade. Delaine was a light weight wool or wool and cotton cloth for women's dresses. It was an item for Taylor's fall trade which did not arrive until January.

[11] G. W. Taylor to Joel Parker, Feb. 15, 1853, G. W. Taylor to Josias F. Browne & Co., Feb. 22, March 1, July 18, 1853 (Taylor Letterbooks, I, 142, 158, 161, 250).

[12] G. W. Taylor to John Wingrave, Sept. 2, 1853; G. W. Taylor to Josias F. Browne & Co., Oct. 4, Oct. [n.d.], 1853 (Taylor Letterbooks, I, 270, 278, 282).

a duty of 30 per cent on the manufactured goods, added greatly to the cost and was a major handicap to the movement.[13]

The many difficulties connected with manufacturing, whether it was done in this country or in England, soon convinced Taylor that the only satisfactory solution would be a mill under his own control to make at least the coarser and heavier fabrics so much in demand. He began to work toward this end in 1853, but the great impediment was of course lack of capital. Taylor made a thorough investigation of the possibilities and found that about fifteen thousand dollars would be necessary. At about this time Elihu Burritt, while promoting the cause in England, had enlisted the interest of Harriet Beecher Stowe and her husband Calvin Ellis Stowe. Taylor, taking advantage of this circumstance, wrote to Calvin Stowe summarizing past efforts in the free produce cause and explaining the need for a mill. Taylor hoped for "much aid from his influential exertions."[14]

His first plans for a mill developed so slowly that Taylor often felt deeply discouraged, but at about that time one or two prominent Friends came to him voluntarily, inquired about the mill project, and offered their services in advancing the cause. All these events served to give Taylor fresh hope.[15] Then in May, 1854, he had an opportunity to lease a small mill for $1,180 a year. It would be superintended and operated by the owner, Henry Webster, who would receive $500 for management, $500 for the mill, and $180 for machinery already installed. If $10,000 could be raised, Taylor felt that he could undertake the enterprise and guarantee subscribers 6 per cent on their investment. With this in view he again appealed to Calvin Stowe, who later subscribed $500. Within a short time finances were so encouraging that Taylor went ahead with ordering the machinery.[16] The mill was located in Chester County, Pennsylvania, about forty miles from Philadelphia. Some of the ma-

---

[13] G. W. Taylor to John Wingrave, Feb. 3, 1854; G. W. Taylor to Josias F. Browne, April 24, May 2, 1854 (Taylor Letterbooks, I, 304, 369, 371).

[14] G. W. Taylor to Calvin Ellis Stowe, April 4, 1854; G. W. Taylor to Elihu Burritt, April 8, 1854 (Taylor Letterbooks, I, 352 ff., 357). The Stowes were touring England, where Mrs. Stowe was being received with great acclaim.

[15] G. W. Taylor to Elihu Burritt, April 8, 1854 (Taylor Letterbooks, I, 358).

[16] G. W. Taylor to Calvin E. Stowe, May 12, Oct. 31, 1854; G. W. Taylor to Henry Webster, May 26, 1854 (Taylor Letterbooks, I, 376, 382; II, 41).

chinery was ordered at home, while part of it was imported from England. By early August, Taylor managed to send a few bales of cotton to the mill. Throughout the autumn machinery was received and installed, but delays postponed operations considerably. The total cost of machinery was about $12,000, of which almost $9,000 was subscribed by friends of the cause.[17]

With the beginning of 1855 the mill got fairly into operation under the management of Henry Webster. The plant was equipped for only spinning and weaving, while sizing, bleaching, printing, and other operations had to be arranged for elsewhere. Besides, one B. J. Shreve in Philadelphia did at his mill considerable weaving for Taylor.[18] Even after the essential machinery was in operation, Taylor found that much other equipment was very desirable though not absolutely necessary. Among the later installations was a Jacquard loom on which cotton table damask was woven. Taylor encountered many vexations before this piece was finally installed. A doubler and twister was necessary for making heavy yarns, while a balling machine and a spooling machine were used in the final preparations of knitting cotton and sewing thread respectively. It was also essential to have some machinery for working up wool, since Taylor found it advisable to make mixed wool and cotton cloths (called satinets and cashmerettes) for men's trousers.[19]

At the end of 1856 Taylor was for the first time able to see what the mill had accomplished during a full year's operation. The results were not very encouraging, for there was "some loss." "We only spun about 70 bales the whole year," he added, and the "whole amt of goods recd. from Mill in 1856 is only $9,481.43." Taylor's chief hope was that with all business on a rising market, he might do better in 1857.[20] Business during the spring was quite brisk so that Taylor's stock on hand was appreciably reduced. In the

[17] G. W. Taylor to R. L. Murray, June 12, 1854; *idem* to R. Garsed and Bro., June 24; *idem* to Whiting & Sons, June 29; *idem* to Henry Webster, Aug. 7, Nov. 1; *idem* to R. Garsed, Nov. 7; *idem* to James B. Wright, Sept. 9; *idem* to Elihu Burritt, Oct. 26; *idem* to J. H. Krafft, Nov. 21, 1854; *idem* to Gideon C. Smith, July 7, 1856 (Taylor Letterbooks, I, 385, 394, 396; II, 13, 23, 31, 36, 42, 44, 47, 52, 307).

[18] G. W. Taylor to B. J. Shreve, Dec. 4, 1855 (Taylor Letterbooks, II, 118).

[19] G. W. Taylor to Henry Webster, Dec. 21, 1855, Jan. 10, 1856, Aug. 3, 1857 (Taylor Letterbooks, II, 134 f., 147, 443).

[20] G. W. Taylor to Henry Webster, Jan. 21, 1857 (Taylor Letterbooks, II, 376).

summer of 1857 he requested and was given authority to use $400 of the "wear and tear fund" to put in sizing apparatus at the mill.[21] This was not installed, however.

By the middle of September, 1857, the panic of that year was nearly upon Philadelphia. Since he had no cotton on hand, Taylor decided to close the mill and await developments. On September 25 most local banks suspended specie payment; as a result, Taylor was unable to meet the wages due his hands. He proposed that they take some of the cloth on hand which they could barter in the local stores for groceries. He was anxious for his employees to find other work, especially at farm labor and domestic service, which were yet much in demand. Another problem was deterioration of the machinery if the mill stood idle. Taylor hoped that by keeping two or three employees they could maintain the machinery in running order and finish off the goods in hand.[22]

Since there was very little business during the winter, Taylor spent most of the time in getting his accounts and books up to date. With sales so very slow, he departed from his cash policy and sent goods to a few storekeepers to be paid for as they were able.[23] Not until the spring of 1859 did business begin to pick up appreciably. By this time Taylor's stock of goods was so much reduced that he could plan to reopen the mill. On February 9 he ordered cotton valued at $500, and about April the mill was again in operation. Taylor and Webster curtailed the variety of goods and strove to make only what was certain to sell, so that no large stock would accumulate. The fall trade showed a decided improvement, and the mill remained in full operation.[24] Business continued in a modest way for another year or more. As late as February, 1861, Taylor ordered cotton from Thomas Leech in Memphis. Doubtless the mill had to stop sometime in 1861 because the war had cut off the supply of free labor cotton. In the summer of 1862 Taylor put up the mill machinery for sale.[25]

[21] G. W. Taylor to Calvin E. Stowe, June 15, 1857 (Taylor Letterbooks, II, 433). The "wear and tear fund" was a portion of the capital set aside for upkeep of the machinery.

[22] G. W. Taylor to Henry Webster, Sept. 25, Oct. 2, 12, 1857 (Taylor Letterbooks, II, 469, 473, 479).

[23] G. W. Taylor to Griffith Levering, May 18, 1858; *idem* to Robert Fraizer, Aug. 27, 1858 (Taylor Letterbooks, II, 521, 533).

[24] G. W. Taylor to Thomas Leech, Feb. 9, 1859; *idem* to Henry Webster, April 4, May 23, Nov. 25, 1859 (Taylor Letterbooks, II, 548, 552, 562, 601).

[25] G. W. Taylor to Thomas Leech & Co., Feb. 11, 1861; Condensed

While his chief labors were devoted to the drygoods department, food products had a share of his attention. For sugar Taylor relied chiefly on Robert Lindley Murray, the proprietor of the New York free produce store from 1848 to 1852. He looked after the refining which was done chiefly by "Stuarts." Varieties of sugar are rather bewildering. Among those referred to were, crushed, pulverized, loaf, A, B, C, yellow, and brown.[26] The supply was never steady so that Taylor alternated between having almost no sugar and having an overstock, which required a heavy financial outlay on short notice. R. L. Murray, a young man without wide business experience, sometimes made errors of judgment in handling the sugar trade and often failed to accomplish what was needed. In August, 1852, Taylor was particularly anxious to secure a cargo of Manila sugar, even if the refiners charged a little more for it. A short time later when Taylor had opened his last barrel of sugar he wrote again begging Murray to get fifty barrels of "Laguayra Sugar" which was soon to be sold in New York.[27]

One reason for his shortage at this time was the partial failure of the St. Croix sugar crop. He did succeed in getting some from St. Lucia, and a little later received ten hogsheads of St. Croix sugar. Still his supply was so incomplete that he urged Ezra Towne to ship some by rail.[28] All these vexations led Taylor to send his complaints to the refiners, lamenting "the serious loss to me & sad disappointment to *all* my customers resulting from the failure to furnish a supply of Refined Sugars—I fear [he added] many 'have gone back to walk no more with us' It wd have been better for me to have lost in the River 200 Dolls than to have had this to occur—yes, 500!"[29]

Inventory of Machinery for Sale in Bulk, n.d. (Taylor Letterbooks, II, 633, 651).

[26] G. W. Taylor to R. L. Murray, Aug. 3, 1852 (Taylor Letterbooks, I, 3). The refiners were R. L. & A. Stuart.

[27] G. W. Taylor to R. L. Murray, Aug. 10, 21, 1852 (Taylor Letterbooks, I, 8, 15).

[28] G. W. Taylor to Joel Parker, Sept. 11, 1852; *idem* to George B. DeForest & Co., Sept. 23, 1852; *idem* to Ezra Towne, Oct. 16, 1852 (Taylor Letterbooks, I, 37, 41, 53). The bill for his sugar, including freight and cartage, was $992.28. Shipments from New York Taylor instructed to have sent by sea, by steamboat through the canal, or by railroad, depending on the bulk of the articles and the urgency of his need for them.

[29] G. W. Taylor to R. L. Murray, Oct. 29, 1852 (Taylor Letterbooks, I, 60).

As if this were not trouble enough, Taylor next received an unusually large shipment of sugar which, through either defective refining or improper packing, had a very disagreeable taste and odor. Whereupon Taylor asked Murray how he could

. . . take such a lot of sugar off the hands of the refiner as this lot of yellow and still more . . . send such a quantity of it to me without sending samples— . . . as the sugars were sent to me without seeing them . . . it seems clear to me I am not bound to keep them & therefore object to bearing the loss on them . . . I never wd have suffered the refiner to put shugar in fish barrels or butter barrels, or . . . whatever they are . . . The best I can say now is, . . . let it . . . sell . . . for so much as it may be worth, if not, it is at thy risk, and in the mean time I pay nothing on its account further than the sugar will sell. . . .[30]

Taylor enlisted Elihu Burritt's aid in trying to procure free labor sugar from England, Holland, or France, in the hope of getting it there cheaper in spite of the 30 per cent duty. In discussing the matter Taylor described his present stock and its cost as follows:

Best steam refined crushed, sifted, and pulverized sugar at 7½-8½ cents per lb.
"A" sugar (white soft crushed) 8 cents.
"B" sugar (yellowish ") 7⅝.
Good steam syrup, 40-42 cents per gallon, and no extra charge for barrels or casks.

If an arrangement could be made abroad, Taylor stipulated that he alone must receive such free labor sugar, in order to avoid confusion as to its being a genuine free labor product. Nothing ever came of this project.[31]

In the spring of 1853 Taylor suddenly had thrust upon him $7,000 worth of sugar, which was about twice the amount he expected and consequently tied up his funds. In this predicament he asked Levi Coffin and Joel Parker whether they could help him out either by taking some sugar and molasses, or by advancing money

---

[30] G. W. Taylor to R. L. Murray, Nov. 22, 1852 (Taylor Letterbooks, I, 81). Discussion of this matter continued by correspondence for some months and reached a point of considerable asperity. At the end of Feb., 1853, Taylor had sold about one third of it by mixing it with other sugar.
[31] G. W. Taylor to Elihu Burritt, April 5, 1853 (Taylor Letterbooks, I, 183).

which would be returned to them in fall goods.[32] This unhappy circumstance led Taylor to ask Murray for a clarification of the whole arrangement. He had proceeded on the assumption that Murray charged one-fourth cent per pound for his services in looking after the refining and holding the sugar until needed, just as Taylor himself did in providing the supply of cotton cloth. He asked whether business should proceed on this basis or whether Murray preferred to act merely as an agent. Taylor complained that during a season of low sugar prices Murray was furnishing sugar only at prices so high they would impede sales.[33] Taylor kept up his contacts in St. Croix and bought sugar directly from there as he had opportunity to do so. Early in 1854 he ordered twenty hogsheads of sugar and forty of molasses of the new crop in St. Croix.[34]

Beginning in 1855 sugar became high in price and quite scarce. Taylor was often out of stock completely and experienced many difficulties in this connection. By special effort he managed to obtain a small supply of sugar to tide over the two yearly meeting sessions in April, 1856, but throughout the summer and into "preserving time" in August and September Taylor continued to be almost without sugar. He anticipated that this shortage would cost him $1,000 worth of trade.[35] Even through the panic years of 1857-58 sugar continued to be scarce and relatively high. In fact, after 1855 Taylor never had a really adequate supply of free labor sugar.

Occasionally Taylor referred to his efforts to obtain and sell other products for which there was a limited demand. He was particularly anxious to obtain products from Liberia, since that country was looked upon as the experimental laboratory where the Negro's ability would be proved. Commenting on products received

[32] G. W. Taylor to R. L. Murray, May 25, 1853; *idem* to Levi Coffin and Joel Parker, May 24, 1853 (Taylor Letterbooks, I, 228, 233).

[33] G. W. Taylor to R. L. Murray, Nov. 31 [*sic*], 1852, April 14, 1854 (Taylor Letterbooks, I, 86, 363).

[34] G. W. Taylor to George Walker, March 5, 1853, April 4, 1854 (Taylor Letterbooks, I, 168, 348).

[35] G. W. Taylor to Esther C. Lloyd, Jan. 7, 1856; *idem* to C. H. and W. G. Moore, Jan. 28, 1856; *idem* to Ezra Towne, April 7, 1856; *idem* to R. L. Murray, Sept. 4, 13, 1856 (Taylor Letterbooks, II, 144, 169, 234, 333). Both Orthodox and Hicksite yearly meetings convened at Philadelphia in April. Taylor always had heavy sales at this time to the many out-of-town Friends in attendance.

from Liberia, Taylor wrote that "the last parcel of Coffee though handsome, has not the flavour that pleases my former customers" and suggested starting orchards of the best variety of Java coffee. Taylor was slowly selling Liberia arrowroot "at a low price," but found that druggists refused it because it was not from Bermuda. A short time later he shipped a fan "for cleaning Coffee & Rice" to Liberia. The next year he was receiving small quantities of pepper from Liberia.

In connection with rice, Taylor remarked in 1852 that he was obtaining East India rice, "delivered in my store a trifle under four cents pr lb of good quality & well cleaned."[36] Some of this rice he got through Josias F. Browne in England. In 1853 Taylor established direct contact with a merchant in Calcutta, with the hope of obtaining rice as well as other products. The arrangements were not always satisfactory, for on occasion Taylor had to complain that there "was a great want of care in the selection of the Rice," much of which he found "very poor, dark & dirty"; whereupon he ordered "one ton of the Best quality" with the stipulation that each bag be examined.[37] Spices also figured among the minor food products, but after emancipation in the British colonial possessions the question of supply presented no particular difficulties.

As Taylor proceeded in the work, he more and more felt the need of larger capital. His favorite hope was enlisting the interests of British capitalists sufficiently to insure a large supply of cotton. This dream was never realized to any appreciable extent.[38] When his mill was opened, a separate fund was raised for the purchase of cotton. This helped considerably, but Taylor was seldom able to buy more than from $600 to $1,000 worth of cotton at one order, and he often had to place orders at inconvenient times, such as late spring and summer, when free labor cotton was difficult to get. While machinery for the mill was financed chiefly by subscription, still at the last moment unexpected expenses necessitated Taylor's putting about $2,000 of his own money into it. On later occasions,

[36] G. W. Taylor to S. A. Benson, Nov. 17, 1852, Oct. 31, 1853; *idem* to James Hall, May 30, 1853 (Taylor Letterbooks, I, 75 ff., 236, 284). Benson was the president of Liberia.

[37] G. W. Taylor to Josias F. Browne & Co., March 18, Oct. [n.d.], 1853; *idem* to Henry Libbery, April 5, 1853 (Taylor Letterbooks, I, 175, 187, 282).

[38] G. W. Taylor to Elihu Burritt, April 5, 1853 (Taylor Letterbooks, I, 185 f.).

too, he found it necessary to draw on his other investments to keep the free labor enterprise going.[39] Before the mill began to bring in any returns Taylor was unusually hard pressed. He first tried unsuccessfully to borrow $3,000 on his real estate, and then asked a few of his wholesale customers whether they could advance money to be paid in spring goods.[40] Samuel Rhoads and Richard Richardson acted as trustees for the machinery and cotton funds, so that after 1855 all cotton purchases were made in their names.[41]

Even in its best year (1856) the mill showed a loss rather than any profits. Its closure in October, 1857, of course cut off any hope of profits that year, while rent and interest went on, although many of the subscribers relinquished their claims for payment of interest, and Henry Webster, too, was very considerate. Taylor figured that the eighteen months stoppage ran to an actual loss of nearly $6,000, including that portion absorbed by the subscribers. When the five-year lease expired in 1859, Webster agreed to renew it for one year on the same terms. Later renewals were probably on a one-year basis.[42]

Taylor's relations with the labor employed in his small mill is a matter of some interest. Employment was largely on a family basis, so that men, women, and children were used as operatives. Henry Webster owned the houses which the employees occupied; beyond that the paternalistic system apparently did not operate. Taylor's chief complaint was of imperfections in the weaving. "Floats" and bad selvages were the chief defects. After one or two unhappy experiences Taylor and Henry Webster agreed on dismissing any employees who brought liquor near the mill.[43] Taylor's concern for the welfare of his labor when the mill closed has been alluded to.

The demand for free labor goods is somewhat difficult to assess. Demand would have been greater if the supply had been more

[39] G. W. Taylor to Josias F. Browne & Co., May 7, 1855; *idem* to William Armistead, Nov. 29, 1855 (Taylor Letterbooks, II, 83-85, 104).

[40] G. W. Taylor to Dade C. Street, Nov. 25, 1855; *idem* to Allen Sampson, Nov. 25, 1855 (Taylor Letterbooks, II, 106, 108).

[41] G. W. Taylor to J. H. Krafft, March 25, 1846 (Taylor Letterbooks, II, 226).

[42] G. W. Taylor to Henry Webster, May 23, Sept. 2, 1859 (Taylor Letterbooks, II, 562, 585).

[43] G. W. Taylor to Henry Webster, Feb. 25, 1856 (Taylor Letterbooks, II, 191). "Floats" are filling threads not properly interwoven with the warp.

adequate and satisfactory, while, on the other hand, the supply could have been greatly increased if there had been sufficient demand to justify large-scale operations. Demand for the most part was confined to Quakers—and only a portion of them—, to a few earnest abolitionists of other denominations, and to those influenced by Quaker thought. Chief deterrents were the inadequate and uncertain supply of goods, their inferior quality and higher price, and suspicion on the part of the customers. All, and especially the country folk of the West, constantly questioned the genuineness of free labor goods offered them. They distrusted the clever merchants of the distant and wicked Eastern cities. Hence Taylor had constantly to reassure them on this score.

The best market for free labor goods, even so, was in the West. As early as 1846 Levi Coffin wrote of the growing demand. Up to that time he had resisted importunities to conduct a free produce store because of his own small means and the limited variety of goods available.[44] Taylor's work and the efforts of the Philadelphia Free Produce Association considerably increased the supply, while strict integrity and constant assurances largely overcame suspicion as to the authenticity of goods sold.

Taylor's mail-order business to individuals and groups never assumed very large proportions, but some instances may be noted. To the many inquiries about how to order goods, Taylor responded with minute instructions on how to fill out orders, how to send money, and how to pay shipping charges. He made a practice of selling at wholesale prices to groups of Friends who would unite to send in one large order when there was no free produce store nearby. Individual orders were at retail prices. By April, 1853, Taylor could report that his store "had a pretty brisk trade in our small way this Spring & my stock is considerably broken. . . ." He described his trade as extending through all the Northern states from Maine to Iowa. Among his steady customers were Friends in Columbiana County, Ohio, and members of the Alum Creek (Ohio) Free Produce Association.[45]

[44] Levi Coffin to Samuel Rhoads, Newport, Ind., March 4, 1846; J. M. Thistlethwaite to G. W. Taylor, Millville, N. Y., Nov. 3, 1846 (G. W. Taylor MSS).
[45] G. W. Taylor to Henry Pyle, March 7, 1853; *idem* to Jabez Coulm, March 11, 1853; *idem* to Levi Coffin & Co., April 6, 1853; *idem* to Griffith Levering and Abraham Jackson, Jan. 27, 1853; *idem* to A. S. Leavitt, June 27, 1853 (Taylor Letterbooks, I, 172 f., 189, 131-133, 247).

Taylor's stock of unsaleable and hard-to-sell goods ran high in proportion to his entire business. This entailed much trouble, no profit, and frequent loss. In 1852 he offered Levi Coffin $1,500 worth of satinets at a "very low price," and fifty pieces of printed cotton in seventeen patterns, at 28 cents per yard cash, because, as he explained, "the figures are too large for my customers." The price was low, and, he added, "I think it likely you could do well with them in your location." Taylor had to confess, however, that his stock of unsaleable goods was "constantly increasing," as a result, he feared, of his trying to provide a large variety. This situation was somewhat alleviated after Taylor began to manufacture his own goods.[46]

That most free labor products of all kinds were higher in price than ordinary goods was always one of the great handicaps in the cause, especially in the West, where people, on the whole, had less money to spend. Levi Coffin thought that the first need was for "cheap prints, Calicoes that would cost in Phil from eight to 12 or 14 cents per yd . . . ," while brown muslin was next in demand. One storekeeper in Ohio wrote in 1847 that free labor cotton prints were getting steadily worse in quality and color and would not sell at all. He hoped the Philadelphia association would succeed in improving things.[47] Even when they did so, there were still complaints, as Taylor testified when he wrote:

I am sorry the *new* styles of Prints do not please thee— . . . I got up some time ago a large assortment of the prettiest styles I could— Well the general cry was, they are too *light* and not *plain enough*— Now I have aimed to have them *dark* & *plain* too, & yet they will not do—I believe I shall get the *plain unbleached* muslin & let every one print to her own taste—. . . .[48]

After Taylor's mill got into operation he was able to supply several kinds of goods at market prices, although others had to remain a little higher.[49] Inferior quality was always a great handicap.

[46] G. W. Taylor to Levi T. Pennington, Aug. 16, 1852; *idem* to Levi Coffin & Co., Aug. 16, 1852; *idem* to R. L. Murray, Nov. 31 [*sic*], 1852 (Taylor Letterbooks, I, 12 f., 86).

[47] Levi Coffin to Samuel Rhoads, Newport, Ind., March 4, 1846; W. R. Wheeler to G. W. Taylor, West Elkton, Ohio, May 28, 1847 (G. W. Taylor MSS).

[48] G. W. Taylor to Richard Mann, March 18, 1857 (Taylor Letterbooks, II, 391 f.).

[49] G. W. Taylor to Ezra Towne, Sept. 4, 1852 (Taylor Letterbooks, I, 31).

Defective weaving, ugly patterns, and colors that faded were almost more than even conscientious Quaker women could endure. On this matter Lucretia Mott wrote:

. . . unfortunately, free sugar was not always as free from other taints as from that of slavery; and free calicoes could seldom be called handsome, even by the most enthusiastic; free umbrellas were hideous to look upon, and free candies, an abomination.[50]

[50] Ann Davis Hallowell, *Life and Letters of James and Lucretia Mott*, pp. 87 f.

CHAPTER VI

PROPAGANDA AND THE PRESS

Like all reforms, the free produce movement had its propaganda, chiefly in the form of tracts and journalistic publicity. Newspaper and periodical publications devoted mainly to its advocacy were comparatively few. Journals which gave the free labor principle their endorsement and occasional space in their columns were more numerous, however. Possibly the first newspaper to carry an article condemning the use of slave produce was the *West Chester Recorder* (Pennsylvania) of 1817 or 1818, of which there is apparently no extant file. Its article, "Prize Goods Examined," was copied, however, by the *Philanthropist* of February 7, 1818. This *Philanthropist* was published from August 29, 1817, to October 8, 1818, by Charles Osborn in Mount Pleasant, Ohio. Osborn's conviction that it was wrong to use products of slave labor was stated in his editorial comment on the excerpt from the *West Chester Recorder*.[1]

It was more than two years before this idea again came to the surface in a periodical publication. This time it was the *Emancipator*, published by Elihu Embree at Jonesboro, Tennessee, which, in the issues of July 31 and August 31, 1820, condemned as prize goods the slave and the products of his labor, thereby making the purchaser of those goods "a party in the slave trade."[2]

These first timid voices in the cause were soon to be supplanted by a stronger advocate in the person of Benjamin Lundy. He served his first journalistic apprenticeship under Charles Osborn, for whom he wrote editorials. When Osborn gave up the *Philanthropist* and moved to Indiana, Lundy was to have taken over the paper, but the Missouri question absorbed him and he did not return

[1] *Philanthropist* (Mount Pleasant, Ohio), Feb. 7, 1818. The Quakers' condemnation of war led to their refusal to accept prize goods which were the direct by-product of war. The parallel between slavery and slave labor goods was the original basis from which all later free produce arguments developed.

[2] *The Emancipator (Complete) Published by Elihu Embree, Jonesborough, Tennessee, 1820; a Reprint of the Emancipator, to Which Are Added a Biographical Sketch of Elihu Embree, Author and Publisher of the Emancipator, and Two Hitherto Unpublished Anti-slavery Memorials Bearing the Signature of Elihu Embree* (Nashville, Tenn., 1932), July 31, Aug. 31, 1820, pp. 63, 65.

to Ohio until 1820. There he found Elisha Bates editing the *Philanthropist,* but with scant attention to slavery. Lundy then began to publish the *Genius of Universal Emancipation.* After eight issues in Mount Pleasant, Ohio, he removed it to Greeneville, Tennessee, to fill with his work and his paper the gap caused by the untimely death of Elihu Embree (in 1820) and the cessation of his *Emancipator.*

Between 1822 and 1825 the *Genius* carried three articles from correspondents touching the use of slave labor goods. Not until 1826, two years after his removal to Baltimore, did Lundy begin to give more attention to this subject by putting into his paper news about it.[3] Articles were frequent from then until 1834, by which time the paper had declined because of Lundy's long absence in Texas. During a visit to New England in 1828 Lundy met William Lloyd Garrison, but not until the middle of 1829 did the two become associated in the publication of the *Genius.* Garrison's fiery words soon put him in jail. Thereafter each man went his own way, Lundy to pursue his milder and more cautious program, and Garrison to return to Boston and to begin to publish the *Liberator.*[4]

Even in their brief association Lundy's influence upon young Garrison had been very marked. The early volumes of the *Liberator* strongly reflect the kind of abolitionism Lundy was sponsoring. In the early days Garrison was ready to adopt any form of activity or organization which seemed likely to promote the abolition of slavery. The first volume of the *Liberator* (1831), a weekly of fifty-two issues totaling 208 pages, contains nineteen insertions of all kinds on the free labor subject. These include correspondence, editorials, verse, news items, and advertisements. The second volume (1832) contains nine articles of similar variety; Volume III has twelve, while Volume IV (1834) reaches a total of thirty-four items. Many of these are lengthy discussions of the free labor principle both by those who favored it and by its opponents.[5]

[3] Benjamin Lundy, *The Life, Travels and Opinions of Benjamin Lundy, Including His Journeys to Texas and Mexico; with a Sketch of Cotemporary Events, and a Notice of the Revolution in Hayti,* compiled under the direction and on behalf of his children [by Thomas Earle] (Philadelphia, 1847), pp. 204, 212, 215; *Genius of Universal Emancipation,* II, 84 (Dec., 1822); IV, 61 (Jan., 1825); 111 (Sept., 1825, supplement).

[4] Lundy, *Life, Travels and Opinions,* pp. 28 f.

[5] *Liberator* (Boston), I-IV, *passim* (1831-34).

There can be no doubt of Garrison's attitude toward the principle in these years. His editorial comments were not numerous, but they were emphatic, as the following extracts show:

. . . Slavery is a system of robbery, practised upon millions of our fellow beings— . . . The assertions which have been made are true— that the consumers of the productions of slave labor contribute to a fund for supporting slavery with all its abominations—that they are the Alpha and the Omega of the business—that the slave-dealer, the slave-holder, and the slave-driver, are virtually the agents of the consumer, for by holding out the temptation, he is the original cause, the first mover in the horrid process—that we are called upon to refuse those articles of luxury, which are obtained at an absolute and lavish waste of the blood of our fellow men— . . .

. . . I say, then, that ENTIRE ABSTINENCE from the products of slavery is the duty of every individual. In no other way can our example or influence be exerted so beneficially. How many are there in the free states, who will gladly give a preference for those articles which are not tainted with oppression, even though at first they come a trifle higher than slave products? Let us open a market for free goods, and encourage conscientious planters to cultivate their lands by free labor. . . . Once bring free into competition with slave labor, and the present system of bondage will be speedily overthrown.[6]

Soon, however, Garrison turned his attention more and more to advocating immediate emancipation and denouncing colonization. It is difficult to establish just when he turned wholly away from the free labor principle as a means to advance the abolition of slavery. Certain it is, however, that his reversal had been accomplished by 1847, when he said that abstinence was a waste of time when strong and vital issues were at stake. He further asked, who but the abolitionist was so well entitled to use products of the slave's toil in whose behalf he was laboring? In later years the free labor idea was viewed even with ridicule, when Wendell Phillips Garrison wrote, "The Abolitionists proper, we repeat, although always stigmatized as impracticable, never mounted this hobby as if the battle-horse of victory."[7]

[6] *Ibid.*, I, 65, 121 (April 23, July 31, 1831).
[7] *Non-Slaveholder*, II, 85 (April, 1847); IV, 253 (Nov., 1849); Wendell Phillips Garrison, "Free Produce among the Quakers," *Atlantic Monthly*, XXII, 493 (Oct., 1868). Wendell Phillips Garrison was a son of William Lloyd Garrison.

The *Liberator* ceased about 1840 to be an organ sympathetic to free labor, but another journal, the *Pennsylvania Freeman*, was ready to open its columns to the cause. On August 3, 1836, Benjamin Lundy began to publish at Philadelphia the *National Enquirer and Constitutional Advocate of Universal Liberty*,[8] a general antislavery paper, which carried some free produce news. The first and second volumes contain about fifty articles and notices, most of them advertisements of free produce stores, while the third volume carries seventy such items. Lundy retired as editor on March 8, 1838. On March 15, 1838, the paper appeared as the *Pennsylvania Freeman*, published by the Executive Committee of the Eastern District Anti-Slavery Society of Pennsylvania, under the editorship of John Greenleaf Whittier. During his incumbency, which continued until September 5, 1839, more than three hundred articles, notices, and advertisements appeared concerning the free produce movement. While most of these were advertisements and notices of meetings, the paper carried a full account of the Requited Labor Convention, and had occasional articles of the tract variety, such as "Abstinence from the Fruits of Unrequited Toil," which came from the Buckingham Anti-Slavery Society. From September, 1840, to the end of 1841 the number of free produce notices totaled only 125.[9]

The close of 1841 saw the suspension of the paper as a weekly. The sponsors decided that the money used to sustain it might be better spent on lecturers, and so the paper was to be issued gratuitously from time to time. Under this arrangement five issues appeared between February and October, 1842; none seemed to appear in 1843. By the end of 1843 the Executive Committee of the Eastern District Anti-Slavery Society of Pennsylvania changed its mind again and decided to publish the paper regularly. Beginning in January, 1844, it appeared twice a month under the editorship of J. Miller McKim and C. C. Burleigh. During the next two years 130 items concerned with free produce are to be found in its

[8] Lundy, *Life, Travels and Opinions*, p. 289; *National Enquirer and Constitutional Advocate of Universal Liberty*, Aug. 3, 1836. Most of the information in this chapter has been obtained from the files of the newspapers themselves. An almost complete file of this paper of Lundy's is at the Historical Society of Pennsylvania.

[9] *Pennsylvania Freeman*, 1838-41, *passim*. After Whittier retired from the editorship in September, 1839, the paper was apparently discontinued until September 10, 1840, when publication was resumed under the same auspices. J. Miller McKim was the editor.

columns. Thereafter such material becomes increasingly scarce. The paper finally ceased publication on June 29, 1854.[10]

Meanwhile a paper had arisen in the West to advocate the free produce cause; namely, the *Free Labor Advocate and Anti-Slavery Chronicle* at Newport (Wayne County), Indiana. Publication began as a semimonthly periodical of quarto size in February, 1841. After the first year it became a weekly newspaper, although issues were sometimes irregular. The last issue was that of September 15, 1848. This paper, established to represent the views of radical Friends in Indiana Yearly Meeting, was denounced as a pernicious influence by the conservative leaders. After the separation over slavery in Indiana Yearly Meeting, the paper represented the views of Indiana Yearly Meeting of Anti-Slavery Friends. The editors were Benjamin Stanton, a prominent Friend and local merchant, and Henry H. Way, a physician, both of Newport. The paper contains information on all phases of anti-slavery activity, but devotes much attention to the free produce movement.[11]

Simultaneously with the beginning of the *Free Labor Advocate* another anti-slavery paper was issued from the same press, the *Protectionist*, a semimonthly journal edited by Arnold Buffum, the Rhode Island Friend who was disowned, ostensibly on account of "business troubles" but actually because of his anti-slavery views. He spent the year 1841 at Newport, Indiana, which he made the center of operations for his anti-slavery work. The *Protectionist* contains a relatively small amount of free produce news, but sheds much light on the abolition movement in the West and the reaction of the Society of Friends thereto.[12]

[10] *Pennsylvania Freeman*, Dec. 29, 1841, Jan. 18, 1844, June 29, 1854, and 1841-54, *passim*. The most nearly complete file of the paper, 1838-54, is at the Library Company of Philadelphia. The Library of Congress has an extensive but incomplete file covering 1846-54. During these latter years publication was weekly. Charles Calistus Burleigh (1810-1878) was born in Plainfield, Conn., and early entered abolition activity. He was in Philadelphia when Pennsylvania Hall was burned, and he was later active as an abolition lecturer and editor.

[11] *Free Labor Advocate and Anti-Slavery Chronicle*, 1841-48, *passim*. With the issue of Feb. 25, 1847, the title was changed to *Anti-Slavery Chronicle and Free Labor Advocate*. The only extensive file of this paper is in the possession of Dr. Harlow Lindley, Secretary and Librarian of the Ohio State Archaeological and Historical Society.

[12] *Protectionist*, I, *passim* (1841). Only one volume was published. It was sponsored by the Executive Committee of the Indiana State Anti-Slavery Society. There is a file in the Duke University Library.

The only press organ devoted primarily to the free produce cause was the *Non-Slaveholder*. Begun in 1846 by the leaders of the Philadelphia Free Produce Association, it represented the views of that portion of Philadelphia Friends who inclined to the teachings of Joseph John Gurney. The editors, Abraham L. Pennock, Samuel Rhoads, and George W. Taylor, however, carefully reiterated that "our columns will be closed against every thing of a controversial character relative to difficulties existing in our religious Society. . . ." The prospectus summarized their policy in these words:

Not neglecting any of the other just modes for the slave's liberation, the doctrine of abstinence from the productions of his toil will be prominently held up to view. We regard it as necessary to give the proper force to all proper modes for accomplishing that purpose.[13]

Despite good intentions and a strict avoidance of doctrinal issues, the editors found that the *Non-Slaveholder* met a varied reception throughout the country. Many anti-slavery Friends in the West subscribed to it, but "Body members . . . seam afraid almost to touch it," Levi Coffin reported. Many of them sincerely thought it would only increase divisions within the Society, while some, when they discovered that the editors corresponded with members of Indiana Yearly Meeting of Anti-Slavery Friends, refused on that account to have anything to do with it.[14]

The *Non-Slaveholder* continued under the original editorship for two years. At the close of 1847 Abraham L. Pennock withdrew because of his many other religious and philanthropic interests and his advancing age. During 1848 Samuel Rhoads and George W. Taylor conducted the paper, but at the end of 1848 Taylor ended his editorial duties as the result of his taking over the free produce store earlier that year. In 1849 and 1850 Samuel Rhoads was sole editor. At the close of 1850 the *Non-Slaveholder*

---

[13] *Non-Slaveholder*, I, 2, 40 (Jan., March, 1846).

[14] Levi Coffin to Samuel Rhoads, Newport, Ind., Feb. 8, Aug. 9, March 4, 16, 1846; Samuel Test to G. W. Taylor, Dunlapsville, Ind., March 28, 1846; Benjamin W. Ladd to G. W. Taylor and Samuel Rhoads, Smithfield, Ohio, Dec. 19, 1846; Elijah Coffin to G. W. Taylor, Richmond, Ind., Jan. 26, 1847; Nathan Thomas to Samuel Rhoads, New Garden, Ind., March 22, 1849 (G. W. Taylor MSS). The correspondence gives no indication of opinion in other parts of the country. "Body members" was a term used to indicate members of Indiana Yearly Meeting, as opposed to the seceders organized under the name of Indiana Yearly Meeting of Anti-Slavery Friends.

ceased publication, not, explained the editor, because of "any feelings of doubt or discouragement" as to the free labor principle, nor because of a declining subscription list, but, he added, because

At no period since the day of the Missouri compromise, has the antislavery cause been more deeply involved in gloom, to our view, than at the present juncture. In watching the gradual yielding of the North and the corresponding triumph of the South during the last year, we have seen strong evidence . . . of . . . the influence of northern commerce in the products of slave labor . . . as the grand means by which the slaveholders have accomplished their purposes.

He indicated that other means would be used to disseminate information on the free produce cause.[15]

That other means was, chiefly, the *Friends' Review: A Religious, Literary and Miscellaneous Journal*, begun in 1847 by Enoch Lewis, who continued as editor until 1856.[16] It reflected the more liberal views of those Friends who inclined to Gurney's opinions and for that reason had found the conservative *Friend* unsatisfactory as a religious paper. While not especially advocating the free produce cause, the *Friends' Review* was sympathetic, and printed considerable news, especially annual reports of the various free produce associations. In fact, it is the chief source of information during the three years before the *Non-Slaveholder* was revived.[17] The tracts issued during this period and later by the Ohio Free Produce Association have already been referred to.

Suspension of the *Non-Slaveholder* was particularly disappointing to members of the Free Produce Association of Friends of Ohio Yearly Meeting. Late in 1851 their Managers opened the question of its "resuscitation . . . or the establishment of a small periodical at some suitable point, devoted to the advocacy of free labor." They pushed the matter with the other free produce associations and ap-

---

[15] *Non-Slaveholder*, I, 200 (Dec., 1846); II, 278 (Dec., 1847); III, Supplement (Dec., 1848); V, 269 (Dec., 1850).

[16] Enoch Lewis (Jan. 29, 1776-July 14, 1856), born at Radnor, Pa., was a distinguished mathematician. His own formal education was not very extensive, but through his own efforts he gained wide reputation as a teacher. To this profession he devoted most of his life, teaching at Westtown and other Friends' schools, and conducting schools of his own. He published a number of mathematical texts and also wrote much of a more literary nature. After Enoch Lewis's death, Samuel Rhoads became editor of the *Friends' Review* and continued until about 1867. Publication ceased in 1894.

[17] *Friends' Review*, I-VII, *passim* (1848-54); Elijah Coffin to G. W. Taylor, Richmond, Ind., Jan. 26, 1847 (G. W. Taylor MSS).

pointed a committee to raise one hundred dollars. When these efforts did not bring results, they investigated the matter of publishing a journal themselves. They obtained estimates of the cost, prepared a prospectus, appointed two members to assemble material, decided to call the paper the *Remembrancer*, and set October, 1852, as the time for issuance of the first number. After all these preparations the Managers decided at their meeting, July 10, that they "were not fully prepared . . . to encounter all the difficulties and embarrassments" involved, and so withdrew at the brink. Their annual report recommended that the Association raise two hundred dollars toward the periodical. Their correspondence with Samuel Rhoads on the whole matter induced him to agree to undertake the publication. When arrangements were finally completed, they were to revive the *Non-Slaveholder* under the editorship of William J. Allinson. The Ohio Board of Managers pledged money individually and got other donations to the extent of one hundred dollars. On February 12, 1853, they guaranteed two hundred dollars toward sustaining the paper, provided it was printed on paper of specified size and quality, and provided the expense of publication did not exceed the estimates. George W. Taylor, who, as publisher, had personally assumed financial responsibility for the paper during 1853, demurred at the Ohio Board's restrictions, which, he explained, could not easily be adhered to. Thereupon they were removed, and the money was forwarded unconditionally.[18]

After the paper was launched in January, 1853, the Ohio

[18] Free Produce Association of Friends of Ohio Yearly Meeting, Minutes of the Board of Managers (MS), Oct. 12, Nov. 22, 1851, Feb. 7, March 13, April 10, May 8, July 10, Aug. 14, Sept. 6, Oct. 9, Nov. 13, Dec. 11, 1852, Feb. 12, March 12, 1853; G. W. Taylor to Jonathan Binns, Feb. 18, 1853 (Taylor Letterbooks, I, 153).

Chief among the leaders of the Ohio Free Produce Association was George K. Jenkins (1810-1879), Secretary of its Board of Managers. After teaching for a time at Franklin College, Athens, Ohio, Jenkins settled at Mount Pleasant, Ohio, where he conducted an academy. The Board of Managers of the Ohio Free Produce Association usually met in his schoolroom. Mount Pleasant was a station on the Underground Railroad. Jenkins, David Updegraff (his father-in-law), and other Quaker residents of the town were active in aiding the escape of fugitive slaves (information from Elizabeth M. Jenkins, daughter of George K. Jenkins, in a letter to the author, Jan. 29, 1942).

William J. Allinson was a druggist of Burlington, N. J. He later turned to literary pursuits, of which this was perhaps the first. After Samuel Rhoads's retirement, he became editor of the *Friends' Review* (1867-74). He died on June 11, 1874, and was buried in Burlington, N. J.

Association as well as George W. Taylor and others in Philadelphia pushed subscriptions most vigorously. The policy adopted was to cut the journal to eight pages an issue and reduce the price to fifty cents a year, or clubs of three copies for one dollar, or eight copies for two dollars. Payment was strictly in advance. Subscriptions went quite well; Taylor noted eighty-eight from Salem, Ohio, and remarked that "Some villages in remote sections have sent us more than 50 each," while scarcely any had come from New York City. During 1853 the *Non-Slaveholder* paid expenses and so was continued for another year. The Ohio Association promised financial support if necessary, and the Managers also contributed articles.

During its existence the *Non-Slaveholder* printed practically all available news of the free produce movement, together with much propaganda, which included most of the tracts issued also in pamphlet form. It is therefore the most important single source for the latter part of the movement.[19] Its discontinuance at the end of 1854 was due not to financial failure, but to the fact that Elihu Burritt had been enlisted in the cause. His reputation as a reformer and editor was expected to bring great stimulus to the effort.

During the latter part of 1854 Elihu Burritt was in America. He had already taken a leading part in the free produce movement in England, and was full of enthusiasm. The details are lacking, but by the end of October, 1854, George W. Taylor and others of the Philadelphia association had completed arrangements for publication of Burritt's *Citizen of the World* as successor to the *Non-Slaveholder*. Burritt got out the first number (dated January, 1855) in the preceding month, and early in the new year he returned again to England, where he edited the paper during 1855. In spite of his declared purpose of giving a large portion of his attention to the free produce cause, the first volume of his *Citizen of the World* contains only eighteen articles and notices on that subject. These are nearly all of a general nature or reflect Burritt's own pet project of experimenting with free labor on a plantation in the United States; there is almost no news of the American free produce associations.

George W. Taylor handled all details of publication, while most

[19] *Non-Slaveholder*, I-V (1846-50), N.S., I-II (1853-54), *passim*. Complete files of the first series are to be found at Haverford and Swarthmore colleges. Earlham College has Volumes I-II. The second series is complete at Swarthmore and at the Library of Congress. There are partial files at several other libraries.

of the copy came from Burritt's own pen. With more than three thousand subscribers the first year, the *Citizen* paid expenses with a little to spare. During the latter part of 1855 Burritt was back in the United States. He was much exercised over the question of continuing the paper, for he felt that it had been a complete failure in promoting the reforms he advocated. Burritt finally decided to continue for another year and to press the free labor cause more vigorously.[20] His enthusiasm is reflected by the appearance of thirty-five articles on free produce in the *Citizen* for 1856. A large portion of these concern Burritt's efforts to establish the North American Free Labor Produce Association. Its failure left little incentive to further work. Burritt and Taylor also investigated the extent to which free labor cotton was being grown in Texas by German immigrants. Such favorable reports as they obtained had no practical results. Toward the close of 1856 Burritt proposed to publish a journal to be entitled the *Wealth of Nations*, but that did not materialize, and so ended his attempt to popularize the free produce cause. Here, too, ended all efforts to maintain a journal devoted to free produce; hence news of the movement thereafter is very fragmentary.[21]

There were a few other journals of secondary importance. The most interesting of these is *The Slave; His Wrongs, and Their Remedy*, a small, four-page monthly, begun in 1851 at Newcastle-on-Tyne by British Friends of the free produce cause. During the first two years it was edited by Anna H. Richardson, one of the leaders in England. About 1853 Elihu Burritt took over the journal and was still editing it in 1856.[22] It was devoted chiefly to the free produce cause in England, and carried both news and propaganda articles. The same press also issued a series of tracts, of which the first was *Who Are the Slaveholders? A Moral Drawn from "Uncle*

[20] G. W. Taylor to William Armistead, Nov. 29, 1856 (Taylor Letter-books, II, 104); Elihu Burritt to [G. W. Taylor], New Britain, Conn., Oct. 15, Nov. 13, 29, 30, 1855 (G. W. Taylor MSS); *Citizen of the World*, I, *passim* (Jan.-Dec., 1855).

[21] Burritt's *Citizen of the World*, II, *passim* (Jan.-Dec., 1856). The Library of Congress has a file of Volume I; Duke University has a file of Volume II. Taylor remarked a little later that all losses on both the *Citizen* and *Non-Slaveholder* had come from his pocket (G. W. Taylor to Abner Devol, March 30, 1857, Taylor Letterbooks, II, 399).

[22] *The Slave; His Wrongs and Their Remedy*, Nos. 30, 31, 32, *passim* (June, July, Aug., 1853). There seems to be no extensive file of this journal in the United States. Duke University has the three numbers here listed.

Tom's Cabin," Respectfully Submitted to the Readers of That Work.[23] Another publication was *The Beloved Crime, or the North and the South at Issue: A Friendly Address to the Americans: Also, Some Remarks on the Duty of Encouraging Free Labor Produce.*[24]

It was through Burritt's energetic work in England that Harriet Beecher Stowe, her husband, and her brother became interested in the movement and were induced to contribute to it. At the same time Burritt was also publishing the *Bond of Brotherhood*, which gave considerable attention to free produce, although its chief purpose was to advocate peace and ocean penny postage. In this journal, however, for July, 1853, Burritt published his "Twenty Reasons for Total Abstinence from Slave-Labour Produce," which succinctly and forcefully stated his position.[25]

A few other papers deserve brief mention. The most important is the *National Anti-Slavery Standard*, which began publication at New York in 1840. Two years later Isaac Tatem Hopper became associated with the publication office, and it was due to his influence that for a time the paper carried considerable free produce news, as well as numerous articles on the difficulties among the Hicksite Friends over slavery. Though less numerous, its items were very similar to those which appeared in the *Pennsylvania Freeman*. Hopper's connection with the paper ended in 1844, and thereafter free produce news sharply declined.[26]

---

[23] This is labeled Newcastle Anti-Slavery Series, No. 1, and is an undated pamphlet of twelve pages.

[24] The title continues: "By the Author of 'A Word on Behalf of the Slave,' and 'Bible Rights of the Slave.'" This tract of forty pages is undated.

[25] *Bond of Brotherhood* was published for a time by Burritt in America, and then transferred to England, where he spent several years. The Library of Congress has a file of Volume I, 1846-47. The journal carried no free produce material, apparently, until about 1852 or 1853, when Burritt began to push the subject in England. No file for the later years has been found by the writer. Burritt's *Twenty Reasons* ... was also published as a pamphlet at Bucklersbury, n.d. Duke University has it in pamphlet form. *Burritt's Christian Citizen*, a weekly newspaper which he published from 1846 to 1850 in Worcester, Mass., contains only two editorials and one other article on free labor. The financial failure of this paper left Burritt considerably in debt. The Library of Congress has an extensive but incomplete file of this paper.

[26] *National Anti-Slavery Standard*, 1840-46, *passim*. The circumstances of the founding and early history of this paper are discussed in Gilbert Hobbs Barnes, *The Antislavery Impulse, 1830-1844* (New York, 1933), p. 173.

Freedom's Journal, published at New York, 1827-29, was one of the early papers edited by Negroes. It contained several articles on the economic advantages of free labor. One editorial was entitled "What Does Your Sugar Cost?" In 1850 the *Impartial Citizen,* published at Syracuse, New York, by Henry H. Garnett, a Negro, carried a long article denouncing the use of slave labor goods. The *Vergennes* (Vermont) *Citizen* during the 1850's contained some material, chiefly the writing of Henry Miles, previously referred to. In Ohio three papers were induced to give some space to the cause through the efforts of the Ohio Free Produce Association: the *Herald of Freedom* published at Wilmington, the *Ohio Columbian* published at Columbus, and the *Oberlin Evangelist.* The first two were newspapers. During 1853-55 the *Ohio Columbian* carried only three or four articles. Between 1853 and 1856 the *Oberlin Evangelist* published seventeen articles, chiefly contributions from members of the Ohio Free Produce Association.[27]

Tract material and pamphlet publications have been referred to elsewhere, and discussion of them is not needed here. After the suspension of *Burritt's Citizen of the World* in 1856, the *Friends' Review* and the *Friends' Intelligencer* were the only journals carrying any news of the free produce cause. Consequently, any connected story of the movement must cease with 1856. Doubtless much more pamphlet literature and other ephemerata were published than that herein cited. Much of it, as well as the original records of the associations and correspondence of their officers, has been lost. The propaganda is largely repetitious and bulks large in proportion to news of the movement.

Very few leaders in the free produce movement achieved widespread notoriety in the advocacy of the cause. Like the early antislavery movement, the free produce cause was sponsored by plain people with small financial resources who, for the most part, did not give their full time to or make their living by reform work. Neither was their journalism headed by men of nation-wide recognition. The few exceptions may be noted.

[27] *Freedom's Journal,* New York City, 1827-29, *passim.* The editors were Samuel E. Cornish and John B. Russwurm. Files of the Ohio papers are located as follows: *Herald of Freedom* at the Western Reserve Historical Society; *Ohio Columbian* at the Ohio State Archaeological and Historical Society; *Oberlin Evangelist* (for these years) at Syracuse University. The *Vergennes Citizen* is at the Bixby Memorial Library, Vergennes, Vt., and *Freedom's Journal* at the New York Public Library. There seems to be no extant file of the *Impartial Citizen.*

Among the journalists, Benjamin Lundy and Elihu Burritt have already received attention. John Greenleaf Whittier was undoubtedly the most distinguished writer to give his support to the cause. As editor of the *Pennsylvania Freeman* he gave free produce his unstinted sanction, and upon leaving that journal he said that to succeed in their labors it was necesary for abolitionists "To abandon all traffic in, or use of, the GREAT STAPLE production of slavery, and to disentangle ourselves from all commercial connection with those who traffic in the bodies and souls of men." Whittier endorsed the free produce idea throughout his life, but he never worked actively for it, while the great body of his abolition poems contains nothing on the subject.

The free produce cause had only one poet, Elizabeth Margaret Chandler. She was born at Centre, Delaware, on December 24, 1807, the daughter of Thomas and Margaret (Evans) Chandler, and grew up in Philadelphia under the care of relatives. She was educated at a Friends' school, and at the age of thirteen began to write for publication, although her identity was not generally known. Her writing on slavery attracted the attention of Benjamin Lundy; in consequence, she began to write for the *Genius of Universal Emancipation* in 1826. Three years later she undertook to conduct the "Ladies' Repository" department of that journal. This arrangement continued until the summer of 1830, when Elizabeth Chandler with her aunt and brother moved to Michigan Territory. Here she continued her literary work and her writing for the *Genius*. She died on November 2, 1834, after a long illness described as "remittant fever." Her prose writings consisted chiefly of short essays. They all reflected a highly moralistic viewpoint, and many of them concerned slavery. A series entitled "Letters to Isabel," as well as others, urged the boycotting of slave products. Among her poems on that subject the following excerpts are typical.

THE SUGAR-PLUMS

No, no, pretty sugar-plums! stay where you are!
Though my grandmother sent you to me from so far;
You look very nice, you would taste very sweet,
And I love you right well, yet not one will I eat.

For the poor slaves have labour'd, far down in the south,
To make you so sweet and so nice for my mouth;

The Free Produce Movement

But I want no slave toiling for me in the sun,
Driven on with the whip, till the long day is done.

* * * * * *

Oh Press Me Not to Taste Again

Oh press me not to taste again
Of those luxurious banquet sweets!
Or hide from view the dark red stain,
That still my shuddering vision meets.

* * * * * *

Slave Produce

. . . .

List thee, lady! and turn aside,
With a loathing heart from the feast of pride;
For, mix't with the pleasant sweets it bears,
Is the hidden curse of scalding tears,
Wrung out from woman's bloodshot eye,
By the depth of her deadly agony.

Look! they are robes from a foreign loom,
Delicate, light, as the rose leaf's bloom;

. . . .

Yet fling them off from thy shrinking limb,
For sighs have render'd their brightness dim;
And many a mother's shriek and groan,
And many a daughter's burning moan,
And many a sob of wild despair,
From woman's heart, is lingering there.[28]

The free produce movement was only one of the hundreds of reforms which characterized the nineteenth century. Whether it is viewed as just another crackbrained scheme or as the sincere effort of earnest people, it could scarcely be called a success. Doubtless the work of the free produce societies added its own small part to the avalanche that was abolition; yet that part cannot be accurately gauged. The reasons for failure are more easily arrived at than is

---

[28] Elizabeth Margaret Chandler, *Poetical Works . . . with a Memoir of Her Life and Character*, by Benjamin Lundy (Philadelphia, 1836), pp. 7-44, 108, 111. Most of her poems and essays had previously appeared in the *Genius of Universal Emancipation*.

the extent of achievement. Free produce failed because it made too heavy an economic demand on the individual. Voluntary self-denial can be expected only of the conscientious few, never of the mass. This was the fundamental failure; the theory was perfectly sound. Like popular sovereignty, it never worked out as its advocates anticipated.

The most striking aspect of the free produce cause was its popularity and wide acceptance at the beginning of the abolition movement. Many of the most active abolitionists, like the Welds, boycotted slave labor products individually, but did not advocate that policy publicly. Others, like Gerrit Smith and John Greenleaf Whittier, endorsed the principle throughout their careers. Some, notably William Lloyd Garrison and Stephen Symonds Foster, urged such a boycott in the 1830's, but later abandoned the idea and claimed that abolitionists were especially entitled to use goods produced by the slave whose cause they were espousing.

Among the Society of Friends opinion falls into several categories. First, there was the most radical faction. These Quakers either withdrew from membership individually or joined the organization called Progressive Friends. The people in this category were most active in the free produce movement during the 1830's and the first half of the next decade. After that they became so much involved in political abolition, women's rights, and other reforms that they forgot the free produce movement.

On the other hand, the most conservative Friends kept strictly aloof from all social questions. These were a decided minority. The largest body of Friends may be termed conservatives, who displayed a mild interest in social questions and kept to what they considered a traditional attitude. They condemned slavery, but maintained that the Society of Friends was itself an anti-slavery society, that a verbal condemnation of the institution was sufficient, that any vigorous action would be detrimental to religious spirit and solidarity, and that those members who felt otherwise were "working in their own wills."

Those Friends who led the free produce movement were a compound of the followers of Joseph John Gurney, those radicals who limited their reform interests to the slavery question, and those who refused to let their activity in social questions take them away from the religious fold. Most Friends in this class belonged to many anti-slavery societies during the 1830's and helped to form the various state anti-slavery organizations. About 1840 dissension within the Society of Friends brought a change in the situation. The conservative objections to indiscriminate abolition activity became so strong that most of those involved were forced to make some change in policy. The result was the formation of free produce associations composed exclusively of Friends. This compromise did not bring peace, but it did prevent further ruptures within the Society. The free produce movement was always strongest around Philadelphia. Friends in New York were always loud in their endorsement of the work, but their tangible support was largely lacking. The movement in New England never made much progress partly because of limited numbers. In the West a large body of Friends gave the cause their support, yet the total results were small. Quakers in Ohio and Indiana did not have the money to give any substantial aid in a cause they were sure was right. Total membership in the free produce societies probably did not exceed fifteen hundred. The number of those who made some effort to confine their purchases to free labor goods may have reached five or six thousand. Decline of the movement after 1856 may be charged to the increasing excitement throughout the country. Free produce leaders now saw that abolition would be achieved by more violent means than their quiet policy of boycott. They continued their work, but abandoned the hope of making the boycott of slave labor goods a telling factor in accomplishing the abolition of slavery.

The whole free produce movement, however, contains implications larger than mere differences on the question of slavery. The conflict within the Society of Friends was a matter of fundamental policy rather than an attitude toward a specific reform. Here the free produce movement made its real contribution to Quakerism. While it was by no means the first organized effort of Friends to promote social reform, it was indeed a long step forward. The free produce associations were only forerunners of an evangelical Quakerism which later organized many associations to promote peace, freedmen's aid, education, missions, Indian rights, temperance, and other social reforms. Friends of the free produce associations were a distinct minority, but their earnest, quiet work did much to advance their views throughout the entire body of Quakers. Increasingly, during the latter part of the nineteenth century, Friends gave their attention and effort to social questions, so that when they entered the twentieth century such work was a fixed policy which distinguished them. That policy culminated in the American Friends' Service Committee, which has now a quarter-century's work to its credit. The Friends of the free produce associations, though condemned by many of their fellow members, today stand vindicated. Their convictions are today the policy of the entire Society of Friends, a policy under which a few Friends, deemed radical by the majority of their fellows, can work for their favorite cause without danger of separation, until the cause either dies of inanition or wins to it the whole body of Friends.

APPENDIX

Chronological List of Free Produce Societies
(With an indication of the extant records of each)

Date of Founding	Name of Society	Place	Date When Last Known
1826 (June)	Wilmington Society for the Encouragement of Free Labor (Constitution; Report, 1827)	Wilmington, Del.	1827
1826 (Sept.)	Free Produce Society of Pennsylvania (Constitution; Notices, 1827-29, 1831-32, 1837)	Philadelphia, Pa.	1837
1829 (Jan.)	Female Association for Promoting the Manufacture and Use of Free Cotton (Reports, 1829-32)	Philadelphia, Pa.	1832
1830 (Dec.)	Colored Men's Free Produce Association (Notices, 1831)	Philadelphia, Pa.	1831
1830 (Dec.)	Colored Female Free Produce Society (Notices, 1831)	Philadelphia, Pa.	1831
1832	Green Plain Free Produce Society (Report, 1833)	Clark County, Ohio	1836
1833	Oxford Anti-Slavery and Free Produce Society, which in 1838 became the Union Free Produce Society (Constitution; Reports, 1839-42, 1844-45)	Chester County, Pa.	1845
1833	Harrisville Free Produce and Anti-Slavery Society of Harrison County (Report, 1833)	Harrison County, Ohio	1833
1834	Free Produce and Anti-Slavery Society of Monroe County, Ohio (Preceded by the Aiding Abolition Society of Monroe County, Ohio, formed in 1826) (Report, 1834)	Monroe County, Ohio	1834
1837	Association of Friends for Promoting the Abolition of Slavery and Improving the Condition of the Free People of Color (Constitution; Reports, 1846-51)	Philadelphia, Pa.	1851
1838	American Free Produce Association (Constitution; Reports, 1837-47)	Philadelphia, Pa.	1847
1842 (Jan.)	Wayne County Free Produce Association (Constitution; Notices, 1841-42, 1850)	Wayne County, Ind.	1850
1842 (Feb.)	Western Free Produce Association (Constitution; Reports, 1842-49)	Western Ohio and Eastern Indiana	1849
1842	Marion County Free Produce Association (Constitution; Report, 1842)	Whetstone, Ohio	1842
1842[?]	Western New York Free Produce Association (Notice, 1842)	Wayne County, N. Y.	1842
1845 (May)	Free Produce Association of Friends of New York Yearly Meeting (Constitution; Reports, 1845-55)	New York City	1855

Chronological List of Free Produce Societies
(Continued)

Date of Founding	Name of Society	Place	Date When Last Known
1845 (June)	Free Produce Association of Friends of Philadelphia Yearly Meeting (Constitution; Reports, 1845-54; Notices, 1855-56; Minutes of Board of Managers, 1845-52)	Philadelphia, Pa.	1856
1846	Free Produce Association of Friends of Ohio Yearly Meeting (Constitution; Reports, 1849-55; Notices, 1858-59; Minutes of Board of Managers, 1846-57)	Mount Pleasant, Ohio	1859
1846	Iowa Free Produce Association (Preceded by Salem Anti-Slavery Society, formed Feb. 6, 1841) (Notice, 1850)	Salem, Iowa	1860
1848 (June)	Free Produce Society of Friends of New England Yearly Meeting (Reports, 1848-52)	Newport, R. I.	1852
1848	Free Produce Association at Collins and Its Vicinity (Report, 1850; Notice, 1848)	Collins Center, N. Y.	1850
1849	North Carolina Free Produce Association (Notices, 1849, 1851-52)	Guilford County, N. C.	1852
1852	Alum Creek Free Produce Association of Friends (Auxiliary to Free Produce Association of Friends of Ohio Yearly Meeting) (Notices, 1852)	Morrow County, Ohio	1853
[1854]	Free Produce Association of Western Vermont (Report, 1854?)	Ferrisburg, Vt.	[1855]
1855	Free Labor Association of Maine (Notice, 1856)	Manchester, Me.	1856
1856 (May)	North American Free Labor Produce Association (Report, 1856)	Philadelphia, Pa.	1856

Chronological List of Free Produce Stores

Date of Opening	Proprietor	Place	Date When Last Known to Exist
[1817]	Charles Collins	New York City	1843
1825	Jane Webb	Wilmington, Del.	1831
1826	Benjamin Lundy & Michael Lamb	Baltimore, Md.	1827
1829	James Mott	Philadelphia, Pa.	
1829	Fanny Birdsall	Bordentown, N. J.	1829
1829	James L. Pierce	Philadelphia, Pa.	1831
1829	John Townsend	Philadelphia, Pa.	1829
1830	——— Woodward	Egypt, N. J.	1830
1830	Benjamin Lundy	Baltimore, Md.	1830
1830	Lydia White	Philadelphia, Pa.	1846
1830	Amy Pennock	Kennett Square, Pa.	1830
1831	George Truman	Philadelphia, Pa.	1831
1831	A. Laing	Rahway, N. J.	1831
1831	O. Fairfield & Company	Cincinnati, Ohio	1831
1832	Isaac Peirce	New York City	1832
1833	Zebulon Thomas	Philadelphia, Pa.	1835
1833	William Grey & Company	New York City	
1833	Joseph H. Beale	New York City	1835
1834	William Whipper	Philadelphia, Pa.	
1834	Isaac Clement	Philadelphia, Pa.	
1836	S. A. Lewis	Philadelphia, Pa.	
1837	Charles Wise	Philadelphia, Pa.	1843
1837	C. &. E. Adams	Philadelphia, Pa.	
1837	Robert McClure	Philadelphia, Pa.	
1838	William Bassett	Lynn, Mass.	
1838	Charles Cadwallader	Philadelphia, Pa.	
1839	Bishop and Withington	Boston, Mass.	
1839	Clarke and Porter	Philadelphia, Pa.	
1840	Norris W. Palmer	Wilmington, Del.	
1840	Eli & Livezey	Centreville, Pa.	
1841	Levi Coffin & Joel Parker	Newport, Ind.	1844(?)
1841	B. Percival	Philadelphia, Pa.	
1842	Jonathan Macy	Grant County, Ind.	
1842	Seth Hinshaw	Greensboro, Ind.	
1844	J. Park	Philadelphia, Pa.	
1844	Levi Coffin	Newport, Ind.	1847(?)
1846	Thomas S. Field & Company	Philadelphia, Pa.	
1846	Joel Parker	Newport, Ind.	
1846	Joel Fisher	Philadelphia, Pa.	1847(?)
1847	George W. Taylor	Philadelphia, Pa.	1867
1847	Parker and Stanton	Newport, Ind.	
1847	Levi Coffin	Cincinnati, Ohio	1857
1848	L. M. Hoag & George Wood	New York City	1848
1848	Small, Coleman & Co.	Jonesboro, Ind.	
1848	R. L. Murray	New York City	1852
1848	Mount Pleasant Free Labor Co.	Mount Pleasant, Ohio	1862(?)
1849	———	Lynn, Mass.	
1849	Henry Russell	Sandwich, Mass.	
1852	Ezra Towne	New York City	1861(?)
1853	C. M. & M. J. Scarlet	Chester Co., Iowa	
1856	S. Small & E. Brannin	Greensboro, Ind.	
1856	Moses Emery	Saco, Me.	
1856	Alden Sampson	Hallowell, Me.	

BIBLIOGRAPHY

Reference Works

Child, Hamilton (comp.). *Gazetteer and Business Directory of Addison County, Vt., for 1881-82.* Syracuse, N. Y., 1882.

Dictionary of American Biography. Edited by Allen Johnson. . . . New York, 1928-37. 20 vols.

Dictionary of National Biography . . . from the Earliest Times to 1900. . . . London, 1921-39. 25 vols.

Hinshaw, William Wade. *Encyclopedia of American Quaker Genealogy.* . . . Ann Arbor, Mich., 1936—. 3 vols. issued.

Oberholtzer, Ellis Paxson. *Philadelphia; a History of the City and Its People, a Record of 225 Years.* . . . Philadelphia and Chicago [, 1911]. 4 vols.

Oberlin College Library. *A Classified Catalogue of the Collection of Anti-Slavery Propaganda in the Oberlin College Library.* Compiled by Geraldine Hopkins Hubbard. Edited by Julian S. Fowler. Oberlin College Library *Bulletin*, Vol. II, No. 3 [Oberlin, Ohio], 1932.

Simpson, Henry. *The Lives of Eminent Philadelphians, Now Deceased, Collected from Original and Authentic Sources.* . . . Philadelphia, 1859.

Manuscript Collections

Evans, George. Letters from George Evans to his Family and Particular Friends. 1840. Spiceland, Ind. 15 items. (Indiana State Library)

Miles, Henry. Letters and Papers. 1839-85. Monkton, Vt. Approximately 300 items. (Harvard and Duke)

Taylor, George Washington. Letters and Papers. 1809-76. Philadelphia, Pa. 120 items. (These manuscripts are in the possession of Francis R. Taylor of Philadelphia, a great-nephew of G. W. Taylor. They were loaned to the writer.)

———— Letterbooks. 1852-62. Philadelphia, Pa. 2 vols. Letterpress copy of correspondence sent out by G. W. Taylor. The two volumes contain about one thousand pages and approximately seven hundred letters, dealing chiefly with Taylor's free produce business. (Haverford College; Francis R. Taylor, donor.)

Free Produce Societies

Philadelphia. Requited Labor Convention, 1838
  Minutes of Proceedings of the Requited Labor Convention, Held in Philadelphia, on the 17th and 18th of the Fifth Month, and by Adjournment on the 5th and 6th of the Ninth Month, 1838. Philadelphia, 1838. (Library of Congress, Swarthmore College.) (This convention formed the American Free Produce Association.)

American Free Produce Association
  Fifth Annual Report. Philadelphia, 1843. (Haverford)
  Sixth Annual Report. Philadelphia, 1844. (Swarthmore)

Free Produce Association of Friends of New England Yearly Meeting
  Free Produce Meeting. Newport, R. I., June 18, 1850. [broadside] (Haverford)
  Free Produce Meeting. Newport, R. I., June 16, 1851. [broadside] (Haverford)
  Minutes of Free Produce Meeting 6 mo. 17. 1852 at Newport [R. I.] [MS record, together with a printed pledge to use free labor products.] (Haverford)

Free Produce Association of Friends of New York Yearly Meeting
  Reports of the Board of Managers, 4th-10th, 1849-55, New York, 1849-55. [pamphlets] (Duke)

Free Produce Association of Friends of Ohio Yearly Meeting
  Minutes of the Board of Managers (MS). September 11, 1846-January 10, 1857. Mount Pleasant, Ohio. 2 vols.

Free Produce Association of Friends of Ohio Yearly Meeting. Mount Pleasant Free Produce Company
  Account Books. 1852-57. (MS) 2 vols. Day Book. 1842-63 (MS). Inventory of Goods. 1848 (MS). *Articles of Association.* n.p., n.d. [pamphlet] (Western Reserve Historical Society)
  [Printed Reports and Tracts issued by the Association]:
  Extracts from the Minutes of the Annual Meeting of the Free Produce Association of Ohio Yearly Meeting, Held 3d of Ninth Month, 1850, with the Report of the Board of Managers. Constitution, &c. Mount Pleasant, Ohio, 1851. (Oberlin)
  Second Annual Report of the Board of Managers of the Free Produce Association of Friends of Ohio Yearly Meeting Held 9th of Ninth Month, 1851. Mount Pleasant, Ohio, 1851. (Oberlin)
  Address of Farmington Quarterly Meeting (New York) to the Monthly Meetings Constituting it, and to the Members of

the Same, Generally. . . . [Mount Pleasant, Ohio, 1850.] (Oberlin)
Considerations on Abstinence from the Use of the Products of Slave Labor; Addressed to the Members of Ohio Yearly Meeting. . . . [Mount Pleasant, Ohio, 1850.] (Oberlin)
Lewis, Enoch. *Extracts from Observations on Slavery and the Slave Trade.* . . . [Mount Pleasant, Ohio, 1850.] (Duke)
Stolen Goods: or the Gains of Oppression. by Le Mabbett. and Comparison of Stolen Goods with Slave Labor Produce. By Elihu Burritt. [Mount Pleasant, Ohio,] 1850. (Oberlin)
The Plea of Necessity. Mount Pleasant, Ohio, 1851. (Haverford, Oberlin)

Free Produce Association of Friends of Philadelphia Yearly Meeting
Minutes of the Board of Managers (MS), 1845-52. 1 vol. Philadelphia, Pa. (Property of the Friends' Historical Society of Philadelphia; deposited at Haverford College.)

Free Produce Association of Friends of Philadelphia Yearly Meeting
[Printed tracts:]
An Address to Our Fellow Members of the Religious Society of Friends on the Subject of Slavery and the Slave-Trade in the Western World. . . . Philadelphia, 1849. (Haverford, Oberlin)
Circular to Our Fellow Members of the Religious Society of Friends. September 3, 1845. [broadside] (Earlham)

Free Produce Association of Western Vermont
First Annual Report and Address (MS) [ca. 1854], Monkton, Vt. (Duke)

Free Produce Society of Pennsylvania
Constitution. Philadelphia [, 1827]. [pamphlet] (Swarthmore)

QUAKER SOCIETIES

(NOT EXCLUSIVELY FREE PRODUCE)

The Association of Friends for Advocating the Cause of the Slave, and Improving the Condition of the Free People of Colour
Constitution. . . . Philadelphia, 1839.
Annual Reports, 1846-51. Philadelphia, 1846-51.
An Address to the Members of the Religious Society of Friends, on the Propriety of Abstaining from the Use of the Produce of Slave Labour. Philadelphia, 1838.
An Address to the Citizens of the United States, on the Subject of Slavery. . . . [Philadelphia,] 1838.
An Appeal to Females of the North, on the Subject of Slavery. By a Female of Vermont. . . . Philadelphia, 1838.

Extracts from Writings of Friends, on the Subject of Slavery . . . Philadelphia, 1839.
An Address to the Members of the Society of Friends. . . . Philadelphia, 1843.
(All of these tracts are at Swarthmore College.)

OTHER ANTI-SLAVERY SOCIETIES

American Anti-Slavery Society
Proceedings of an Anti-Slavery Convention Assembled at Philadelphia, December 4, 5, and 6, 1833. Philadelphia, 1833.
The Declaration of Sentiments and Constitution of the American Anti-Slavery Society: with an Address to the Public, by the Executive Committee; the Constitution of the United States and also of the Different States Which Are Supposed to Have Any Relation to Slavery. . . . New York, 1837.

American Convention for Promoting the Abolition of Slavery and Improving the Condition of the African Race
Minutes of the Acting Committee (MS), III, 1827-37. (Hist. Soc. Pa.)
Minutes of the Proceedings of a Convention of Delegates from the Abolition Societies. . . . 1794-1837, title and place vary, 1794-1837. [Twenty-six conventions were held.] (Duke, Brown, Library of Congress, Huntington Library)

Anti-Slavery Convention of American Women, 1st, New York, 1837
Proceedings of the Anti-Slavery Convention of American Women, Held in the City of New-York, May 9th, 10th, 11th, and 12th, 1837. New York, 1837. (Oberlin)
An Appeal to the Women of the Nominally Free States, Issued by an Anti-Slavery Convention of American Women, Held by Adjournments from the 9th to the 12th of May, 1837. New York, 1837. (Duke)

Anti-Slavery Convention of American Women, 2d, Philadelphia, 1838
Proceedings of a Convention Held in Philadelphia, May 15-18, 1838. Philadelphia, 1838. (Duke)
Address to Anti-Slavery Societies. Philadelphia, 1838. (Oberlin)

Boston Female Anti-Slavery Society
Report of the Boston Female Anti-Slavery Society; with a Concise Statement of Events, Previous and Subsequent to the Annual Meeting of 1835. Boston, 1836. 2d ed. (Duke)

British and Foreign Anti-Slavery Society
> *Minutes of the Proceedings of the General Anti-Slavery Convention, Called by the Committee of the British and Foreign Anti-Slavery Society, Held in London on the 12th of June, 1840*. . . . London, 1840. (Duke)
> *Proceedings of the General Anti-Slavery Convention, Called by the Committee of the British and Foreign Anti-Slavery Society, and Held in London, from Tuesday, June 13th, to Tuesday, June 20th, 1843*. . . . London [, 1843]. (Duke)
> *Tenth Annual Report*. . . , *May 21st, 1849*. London, 1849.
> *Eleventh Annual Report* . . . , *May 20th, 1850*. London, 1850. (Duke)

Indiana State Anti-Slavery Society
> *Proceedings of the Indiana Convention, Assembled to Organize a State Anti-Slavery Society, Held in Milton, Wayne Co., September 12th, 1838*. Cincinnati, 1838. (Oberlin)

Ohio Anti-Slavery Society
> *Proceedings of the Ohio Anti-Slavery Convention. Held at Putnam, on the Twenty-second, Twenty-third, and Twenty-fourth of April, 1835*. n.p., n.d. (Oberlin)
> *Report of the First Anniversary of the Ohio Anti-Slavery Society, Held near Granville, on the Twenty-seventh and Twenty-eighth of April, 1836*. Cincinnati, 1836. (Duke)

Pennsylvania Society for Promoting the Abolition of Slavery, for the Relief of Free Negroes Unlawfully Held in Bondage, and for Improving the Condition of the African Race
> Minutes (MS), Vol. III (1825-47). Philadelphia. (Hist. Soc. Pa.)

Philadelphia City Anti-Slavery Society
> Constitution. Adopted June 5, 1838, in lieu of one burned in Pennsylvania Hall. (MS Constitution and list of members.) (Hist. Soc. Pa.)

Philadelphia Female Anti-Slavery Society
> *Fifth Annual Report* [for 1838] . . . *January 10, 1839*. Philadelphia, 1839. (Oberlin)

Rhode Island State Anti-Slavery Society
> *Proceedings of the Rhode Island State Anti-Slavery Convention, Held in Providence, on the 2d, 3d and 4th of February, 1836*. Providence, 1836. (Oberlin)

Yearly Meeting Records and Publications

Indiana Yearly Meeting of Anti-Slavery Friends (Orthodox)
 Minutes (MS), 1843-57. Newport (Wayne County), Ind. 1 vol. (Earlham)
 Minutes (printed) 1843-44, 1848-49, 1855 (title varies). [Newport, Ind., 1843-55.] (Earlham)
Indiana Yearly Meeting (Orthodox)
 Minutes. 1823-date. v.p., 1823-. (Earlham)
New York Yearly Meeting (Hicksite)
 Address to the Citizens of the United States of America on the Subject of Slavery, from the Yearly Meeting of the Religious Society of Friends, (Called Quakers) Held in New York. New York, 1837. (Oberlin)
 Address of the Yearly Meeting of the Religious Society of Friends, Held in the City of New-York, in the Sixth Month, 1852, to the Professors of Christianity in the United States, on the Subject of Slavery. New York, 1852. (Swarthmore)
 Memorials Concerning Deceased Friends, Published by Direction of the Yearly Meeting of New York. New York, 1859. (Earlham)
New York Yearly Meeting (Orthodox)
 Address of Scipio Quarterly Meeting of Friends, on the Subject of Slavery, to Its Members. Skaneateles [, 1837]. (Haverford)
Ohio Yearly Meeting (Conservative or Wilburite)
 Minutes, 1854-68. Mount Pleasant, Ohio, 1854-68. (Ohio State Arch. and Hist. Soc.)
Ohio Yearly Meeting (Hicksite)
 Minutes, 1834, 1844-73. Mount Pleasant, Ohio, and other places, 1834-73. (Ohio State Arch. and Hist. Soc.)
Ohio Yearly Meeting (Orthodox)
 Minutes, 1823-61. Mount Pleasant, Ohio, and other places, 1823-61.
Pennsylvania Yearly Meeting of Progressive Friends
 Proceedings . . . , 1853-1905. v.p. (Swarthmore)
Philadelphia Yearly Meeting (Hicksite)
 An Address to the Quarterly, Monthly and Preparative Meetings, and the Members thereof, Composing the Yearly Meeting of Friends, Held in Philadelphia, by the Committee Appointed at the Late Yearly Meeting to Have Charge of the Subject of Slavery. New York, 1839. (Library of Congress, Haverford)
 Western Quarterly Meeting: To the Members of the Society of Friends in Pennsylvania and Elsewhere. Tenth month, 18, 1845. Philadelphia, 1845. (Haverford)

Philadelphia Yearly Meeting (Orthodox)
Minute on Slavery, 1839. n.p., n.d. [broadside]
(Earlham, Library of Congress)
Philadelphia Yearly Meeting of Women Friends
Minutes, 1688-1813 (MS). Philadelphia. 1 vol. (Arch Street Center, Philadelphia)
Philadelphia Yearly Meeting of Women Friends (Hicksite)
Extracts from the Minutes . . . , 1840, 1854. Philadelphia, 1840, 1854. (Earlham)

Pamphlets and Broadsides

An Address to the People of Great Britain on the Propriety of Abstaining from West India Sugar and Rum. . . . Philadelphia, 1792. 10th ed. with additions. (Haverford, Swarthmore)

Bassett, William. *Proceedings of the Society of Friends in the Case of William Bassett.* Worcester, Mass., 1840. (Duke)

The Beloved Crime, or the North and the South at Issue: A Friendly Address to the Americans. Also, Some Remarks on the Duty of Encouraging Free Labour Produce. By the Author of "A Word on Behalf of the Slave," and "Bible Rights of the Slave." London, n.d. (Duke)

Burritt, Elihu. *Twenty Reasons for Total Abstinence from Slave-Labour Produce.* [London, 1853.] (Duke)

Considerations Addressed to Professors of Christianity of Every Denomination, on the Impropriety of Consuming West-India Sugar and Rum, as Produced by the Oppressive Labour of Slaves. London [, 1792]. (Mercantile Library Company, Philadelphia)

Crafton, William Bell. *A Short Sketch of the Evidence, Delivered before a Committee of the House of Commons for the Abolition of the Slave Trade: To Which Is Added a Recommendation of the Subject to the Serious Attention of People in General.* London, 1792. (Haverford)

Edmunds, Lucy. *A Short Sketch of the Life of Our Dear Friend John Horn: With Some of His Expressions towards His Close. By Lucy Edmunds. Also, Considerations on the African Slave Trade and the Use of West India Produce. First Published by Him in His Last Illness.* London, 1806. (Duke)

Free Labor Cotton Depot. [London, 1853? broadside] (Swarthmore)

Gunn, Lewis C. *Address to Abolitionists.* Philadelphia, 1838. (Duke)

Henderson, B. *East India Sugar Basins.* [London, 1791? broadside] (Swarthmore)

Hicks, Elias. *Observations on the Slavery of the Africans and Their Descendants, and on the Use of the Produce of Their Labour.* Philadelphia, 1823. 3d ed. (Haverford)

Hodgson, Adam. *A Letter to M. Jean-Baptiste Say, on the Comparative Expense of Free and Slave Labour.* Liverpool, New York, 1823. (Hist. Soc. Pa., Univ. of N. C.)

Horn, John. *Some Considerations on the African Slave Trade, and the Use of West India Produce.* January 17, 1805. [London, 1805. broadside] (Haverford)

Hurnard, James. *The True Way to Abolish Slavery.* London, n.d. (Duke)

Lewis, Graceanna. *An Appeal to Those Members of the Society of Friends Who, Knowing the Principles of the Abolitionists, Stand Aloof from the Anti-Slavery Enterprise.* n.p., n.d. (Haverford)

Marriott, Charles. *An Address to the Members of the Religious Society of Friends, on the Duty of Declining the Use of the Products of Slave Labour.* New York, 1835. (Duke, Swarthmore)

Mifflin, Warner. *The Defence of Warner Mifflin Against Aspersions Cast on Him on Account of His Endeavors to Promote Righteousness, Mercy and Peace, among Mankind.* Philadelphia, 1796. (Duke)

Pease, Joseph, Sen. *A Letter from Joseph Pease, Sen., Addressed to Jonathan Backhouse, of Darlington, both Members of the South Durham British India Society, on the Subject of the Slave Trade and Slavery.* May 11, 1842, Darlington, September 5, 1842. [broadside] (Haverford)

[Rhoads, Samuel.] *Considerations on the Use of the Productions of Slavery, Addressed to the Religious Society of Friends.* Philadelphia, 1844. (Haverford, Duke, Library of Congress)

Sugar from Another Hemisphere. n.p., n.d. [November 24, 1830? broadside] (Duke)

Periodicals and Newspapers

The Abolitionist: or Record of the New-England Anti-Slavery Society. Boston, Vol. I, Jan.-Dec., 1833. monthly. (No more published.)

American Free Produce Journal. Philadelphia, Vol. I, No. 1, Oct., 1842. (Apparently no more published.) (Hist. Soc. Pa.)

Anti-Slavery Bugle. Salem, Ohio, 1845-61. weekly newspaper. (Ohio State Arch. and Hist. Soc.)

The Berean: A Religious Publication. Wilmington, Del. Vols. I-III, 1824-27; N.S. Vol. I, 1827-28. monthly (Guilford College)

The British Friend: A Monthly Journal, Chiefly Devoted to the Interests of the Society of Friends, Glasgow, Vols. I-XLIX, 1843-91; N.S. Vols. I-XXI, 1892-1912.

Burritt's Christian Citizen. Worcester, Mass., 1844-50. weekly newspaper. (Library of Congress)

Burritt's Citizen of the World. Philadelphia, Vols. I-II, 1855-56. monthly. (Vol. I at Library of Congress; Vol. II at Duke)

The Emancipator (Complete) Published by Elihu Embree, Jonesborough, Tennessee, 1820; a Reprint of the Emancipator, to Which Are Added a Biographical Sketch of Elihu Embree, Author and Publisher of the Emancipator, and Two Hitherto Unpublished Anti-Slavery Memorials Bearing the Signature of Elihu Embree. Nashville, Tenn., 1932. monthly.

Free Labor Advocate and Anti-Slavery Chronicle. Newport (Wayne County), Ind., 1841-48. Vol. I published semimonthly as a periodical; the remainder is a weekly newspaper. (File owned by Dr. Harlow Lindley)

Freedom's Journal. New York City, 1827-29. weekly newspaper. (N. Y. Public Library; film copy at Duke)

The Friend: A Monthly Journal. London, Vols. I—, 1843-date.

The Friend: A Religious and Literary Journal. Philadelphia, Vols. I—, 1827-date. (Orthodox) weekly.

The Friend; or, Advocate of Truth: A Religious Publication. Philadelphia, Vols. I-IV, 1828-33. (Hicksite) monthly.

Friends' Intelligencer. Philadelphia, Vols. I—, 1838-date. (Hicksite) weekly.

Friends' Review: A Religious, Literary and Miscellaneous Journal. Philadelphia, Vols. I-XLVIII, 1848-94. (Orthodox) weekly.

Genius of Universal Emancipation. Mount Pleasant, Ohio, Jonesboro, Tenn.; Baltimore, Md.; Washington, D. C.; Philadelphia, Pa., Vols. I-XVI, 1821-39. monthly and weekly. (Boston Public Library)

The Liberator. Boston, 1831-65. weekly newspaper.

National Anti-Slavery Standard. New York City, 1840-50. weekly newspaper.

National Enquirer and Constitutional Advocate of Universal Liberty. Philadelphia, 1836-38. weekly newspaper. Becomes *Pennsylvania Freeman.* (Hist. Soc. Pa.)

National Era. Washington, D. C., 1847-60. weekly newspaper.
Non-Slaveholder. Philadelphia, Vols. I-V, 1846-50; N.S., Vols. I-II, 1853-54. monthly. (Earlham, Haverford, Swarthmore, Brown, Library of Congress)
Oberlin Evangelist: A Semi-monthly Periodical Devoted to the Promotion of Religion. Sustained by an Association, Oberlin, Ohio, Vols. I-XXIV, 1838-62. (Syracuse Univ.)
Ohio Columbian. Columbus, Ohio, 1853-56. weekly newspaper. (Ohio State Arch. and Hist. Soc.)
Pennsylvania Freeman. Philadelphia, 1838-54. weekly, semimonthly, etc. newspaper. (Hist. Soc. Pa., Library Company of Phila., Library of Congress)
Philanthropist. Mount Pleasant, Ohio, 1817-18. weekly newspaper. (Ind. State Lib.)
Protectionist. New Garden (Wayne County), Ind., Vol. I, Jan.-Dec., 1841. semimonthly. (No more published) (Duke)
The Slave; His Wrongs and Their Remedy. Newcastle-on-Tyne, England, [1851-56?]. monthly. (Duke)
Vergennes Citizen. Vergennes, Vt., 1855-57. weekly newspaper. (Bixby Memorial Library, Vergennes, Vt.)
Voice of Freedom. Montpelier, Vt., 1839-40. weekly newspaper. (Duke)
Western Friend. Cincinnati, Vols. I-II, 1847-49. monthly (Earlham)

BIOGRAPHY, CORRESPONDENCE, AND TRAVELS

Allen, William. *Life of William Allen, with Selections from His Correspondence.* London, 1846. 3 vols.
[Branagan, Thomas.] *The Guardian Genius of the Federal Union; or, Patriotic Admonitions on the Signs of the Times, in Relation to the Evil Spirit of Party, Arising from the Root of All Our Evils, Human Slavery: Being Part of the Beauties of Philanthropy.* By a Philanthropist. New York, 1840. 2d ed.
Brissot de Warville, Jacques Pierre. *New Travels in the United States of America. Performed in 1788. Translated from the French.* London, 1792. Reprinted in Great American Historical Classics Series, Bowling Green, Ohio, 1919. (Ohio State Univ.)
Burritt, Elihu. *The Learned Blacksmith: The Letters and Journals of Elihu Burritt.* Edited by Merle Curti. New York, 1937.
Chandler, Elizabeth Margaret. *Poetical Works . . . with a Memoir of Her Life and Character.* By Benjamin Lundy. Philadelphia, 1836. (Duke)

Clarkson, Thomas. *The History of the Rise, Progress, and Accomplishment of the Abolition of the African Slave-Trade by the British Parliament.* London, 1808. 2 vols.

Coffin, Levi. *Reminiscences of Levi Coffin, the Reputed President of the Underground Railroad; Being a Brief History of the Labors of a Lifetime in Behalf of the Slave, with Stories of Numerous Fugitives, Who Gained Their Freedom through His Instrumentality, and Many Other Incidents.* Cincinnati [, 1876].

Edgerton, Walter. *History of the Separation in Indiana Yearly Meeting of Friends; Which Took Place in the Winter of 1842 and 1843, on the Anti-slavery Question; . . . Embracing the Documents Issued by Both Parties Relative Thereto. . . .* Cincinnati, 1856. (Duke)

From under His Wings: A Sketch of the Life of Robert Lindley Murray. New York, 1876. (Haverford)

Hallowell, Ann Davis. *James and Lucretia Mott: Life and Letters.* Edited by their Granddaughter. . . . Boston, 1884.

Hicks, Elias. *Letters of Elias Hicks: Including also Observations on the Slavery of the Africans and Their Descendants, and on the Use of the Produce of Their Labor.* Philadelphia, 1861.

Imlay, Gilbert. *A Topographical Description of the Western Territory of North America: Containing a Succinct Account of Its Soil, Climate, Natural History, Population, Agriculture, Manners and Customs, in a Series of Letters to a Friend in England.* Dublin, 1793. Reprinted in Great American Historical Classics Series, Bowling Green, Ohio, 1919. (Ohio State Univ.)

Jefferson, Thomas. *The Writings of Thomas Jefferson. . . .* Washington, 1904. 20 vols.

Justice, Hilda (comp.). *Life and Ancestry of Warner Mifflin: Friend—Philanthropist—Patriot.* Philadelphia, 1905.

Lewis, Joseph L. *A Memoir of Enoch Lewis.* West Chester, Pa., 1882. (Guilford)

Lundy, Benjamin. *The Life, Travels and Opinions of Benjamin Lundy, Including His Journeys to Texas and Mexico; with a Sketch of Cotemporary Events, and a Notice of the Revolution in Hayti.* Compiled under the direction and on behalf of his children [by Thomas Earle]. Philadelphia, 1847. (Duke)

New York Association of Friends for the Relief of those Held in Slavery, &c. *Testimony . . . concerning Charles Marriott, Deceased.* New York, 1844. (New York Depository of Friends' Records)

Osborn, Charles. *Journal of That Faithful Servant of Christ, Charles Osborn, Containing an Account of Many of His Travels and Labours in the Work of the Ministry, and His Trials and Exercises in the Service of the Lord, and His Defence of the Truth, as It Is in Jesus.* Cincinnati, 1854. (Earlham, Guilford)

[Pennsylvania Hall Association.] *History of Pennsylvania Hall, Which Was Destroyed by a Mob, on the 17th of May, 1838.* ... Philadelphia, 1838. (Swarthmore)

Shore, William Teignmouth. *John Woolman; His Life and Our Times; Being a Study in Applied Christianity.* London, 1913.

Sturge, Joseph. *A Visit to the United States in 1841.* Boston, 1842.

Taylor, George Washington. *Autobiography and Writings.* ... Philadelphia, 1891. (Earlham)

Vaux, Roberts. *Memoirs of the Lives of Benjamin Lay and Ralph Sandiford; Two of the Earliest Public Advocates for the Emancipation of the Enslaved Africans.* Philadelphia, 1815.

Woolman, John. *The Journal and Essays of John Woolman.* Edited from the Original Manuscripts with a Biographical Introduction, by Amelia Mott Gummere. Philadelphia and London, 1922.

Secondary Works

Adams, Alice Dana. *The Neglected Period of Anti-Slavery in America, 1808-1831.* Boston, 1907. Radcliffe College Monographs, No. 14.

Alexander, Arthur C. *Koloa Plantation, 1835-1935: A History of the Oldest Hawaiian Sugar Plantation.* Honolulu, 1937.

Boggess, Arthur Clinton. *The Settlement of Illinois, 1778-1830.* Chicago, 1908. Chicago Historical Society's Collection, Vol. V.

Drake, Thomas Edward. "Northern Quakers and Slavery." Typewritten doctoral dissertation, Yale University, 1933.

Garrison, Wendell Phillips. "Free Produce among the Quakers," *Atlantic Monthly*, XXII, 485-494 (October, 1868).

Janney, Samuel Macpherson. *An Examination of the Causes Which Led to the Separation of the Religious Society of Friends in America, in 1827-28.* Philadelphia, 1868.

Locke, Mary Stoughton. *Anti-Slavery in America from the Introduction of African Slaves to the Prohibition of the Slave Trade (1619-1808).* Boston, 1901. Radcliffe College Monographs, No. 11.

Russell, Elbert. *The History of Quakerism.* New York, 1942.

Thomas, Allen C., and Richard Henry Thomas. *A History of the Friends in America.* Philadelphia, 1930. 6th ed.

Wilkinson, Norman B. "The Philadelphia Free Produce Attack upon Slavery," *Pennsylvania Magazine of History and Biography*, LXVI, 294-313 (July, 1942).

INDEX

Abolition movement, characteristics of, 30; in Indiana, 48 f.; in Pennsylvania, 23 f.; political aspects of, 30; Quaker attitude toward, 4, 104, 114 f.

Abolitionists, adopt free produce idea, 21, 59, 114; claim special right to use slave labor goods, 102, 114; criticized for not promoting free produce movement, 28 f.; reasons for not promoting it, 25 n.

Abstinence from use of slave labor goods. *See* Slave labor goods

Adams, C. & E., 119

Africa, quality of cotton produced in, 76; source of free labor products, 76, 80. *See also* Algeria, Liberia, South Africa

African imphee (sorghum cane), 80

Aiding Abolition Society of Monroe County, Ohio, 117; endorses free produce cause, 19

Alabama, 75; source of free labor cotton, 65, 74

Alexander I, Emperor of Russia, 8 n.

Algeria, source of free labor cotton, 76

Allen, William, abstains from use of sugar, 8

Allinson, Samuel, 36

Allinson, Samuel, Jr., 65 n.

Allinson, William J., 107 n.; edits *Non-Slaveholder*, 107 f.

Alsop, Samuel, 36, 65 n.

Alum Creek Free Produce Association (Morrow Co., Ohio), 50 n., 56, 97, 118

American Anti-Slavery Society, 19, 21; fails to understand free produce movement, 25 n.

American Convention for Promoting the Abolition of Slavery and Improving the Condition of the African Race, adopts resolutions condemning use of slave labor products, 11 f.; investigates sources of free labor products, 16, 60 f.; meetings of, 11 f., 18; notes increasing demand for slave labor goods, 12; offers prize for demonstration of free and slave labor costs, 12

American Free Produce Association, 20, 50, 57, 58 f., 117; ceases to manufacture cotton cloth, 29; J. Miller McKim is agent for, 81; Lydia White is agent for, 81; manufactures free labor goods, 63 f.; meetings of, 26-28; organized, 24 f.; promotes free produce cause among anti-slavery societies, 27; seeks free labor cotton, 62

American Free Produce Journal (Philadelphia), 28

American Friends' Service Committee, 116

Anti-Slavery Convention of American Women, urges boycott of slave labor goods, 22

Anti-Slavery Convention of the World. *See* General Anti-Slavery Conventions (London, 1840, 1843)

Anti-slavery movement, characteristics of before 1831, 30

Anti-Slavery Society of Ferrisburgh (Vt.) and Vicinity, 46

Anti-Slavery Society of Maryland, endorses boycott of slave labor goods, 12

Anti-Slavery Society of Pennsylvania, Executive Committee of the Eastern District, publishes *Pennsylvania Freeman*, 103

Antigua (West Indies), 8

Arkansas, Nathan Thomas visits, 72; source of free labor products, 72

Arrowroot, produced by free labor, in Liberia, 95

Association of Friends for Promoting the Abolition of Slavery and Improving the Condition of the Free People of Colour, 28, 34 f., 117; Committee on Requited Labor of, 35

Atlee, Edwin P., 14, 15 n.

Australia, source of free labor cotton, 76

Autauga Co., Ala., displays hostility toward the North, 75

Authenticity of free labor goods. *See* Free labor goods

Baltimore, Md., 101; free produce stores in, 81, 119

[133]

Baptist Church, 3, 30
Barbados (West Indies), 79; slavery in, 5
Barton, Isaac, 12, 14, 15 n.
Bassett, William, 25, 26 f., 27 n., 119
Beale, Joseph H., conducts free produce store, 80 f., 81 n., 119
Beard, William, 51
Benedict, Aaron Lancaster, 50
Benezet, Anthony, 5 n.
Bermuda, condition of Negroes in, 79
Betts, William C., 23, 25
Birdsall, Fanny, 119
Bishop and Withington, 119
Bloomfield, Joseph, 11 n.
Board of Managers, of Free Produce Association of Friends of New York Yearly Meeting, 42-44
Board of Managers, of Free Produce Association of Friends of Ohio Yearly Meeting, effect of Wilbur-Gurney controversy on, 52; interests anti-slavery periodicals in free produce cause, 56, 111; leads in reviving *Non-Slaveholder*, 54 f., 106 f.; members to write articles for *Non-Slaveholder*, 55; organizes Mount Pleasant Free Produce Company, 52; promotes free produce cause at Oberlin College, 55; proposes publishing a periodical, 54 f.; supports *Burritt's Citizen of the World*, 56
Board of Managers, of Philadelphia Free Produce Association, 36, 78, 85; buys "cottage gin," 73; changes name of Association, 37; committees of, 65 n.; desires to aid nonslaveholding farmers, 72; members of, 36; reports of, 37, 68 f.; transfers business to G. W. Taylor, 38
"Body members," defined, 105 n.
Bond of Brotherhood (Elihu Burritt, ed.), 110; location of file of, 110 n.
Bordentown, N. J., 119
Boston, Mass., 76, 78, 101; free produce stores in, 81, 119
Boston Sugar Refinery, 78
Bouvier, John, 14, 15 n.
Boycott of slave labor goods, 57, 59; adopted by Indiana Yearly Meeting of Anti-Slavery Friends, 34; first American society for the, 13; in Great Britain (1791), 9 f. *See also* Free produce movement, Free produce societies.
Branagan, Thomas, condemns use of West Indian products, 8 f.
Brannin, E., 119
Brissot de Warville, Jacques Pierre, predicts use of maple sugar, 10
British and Foreign Anti-Slavery Society, Address published, 53 n.
British India Society, 40
Brosius, William, 20 n.
Browne, Josias F., and Co., British cotton manufacturers, 58, 87, 95
Buckingham (Pa.) Anti-Slavery Society, 103
Buffum, Arnold, disowned for anti-slavery views, 31 n., 104; edits *Protectionist*, 104
Burleigh, Charles Calistus, 25, 104 n.; edits *Pennsylvania Freeman*, 103 f.
Burlington, N. J., residence of G. W. Taylor, 84
Burritt, Elihu, 39, 46, 55, 108, 112; author of "A Comparison of stolen goods with slave labor produce," 53 n.; edits *Bond of Brotherhood*, 110; edits *Burritt's Christian Citizen*, 110 n.; edits *Citizen of the World*, 108; edits *The Slave; His Wrongs and Their Remedy*, 109; leads British free produce movement, 57, 89, 108, 110; publishes "Twenty Reasons for Total Abstinence from Slave Labour Produce," 110
Burritt's Christian Citizen (Worcester, Mass.), 110 n.; location of file of, 110 n.
Burritt's Citizen of the World, 56, 108 f., 111; location of files of, 109 n.; publicizes free produce movement, 109
Byhalia, Marshall Co., Miss., source of free labor cotton, 71

Cadwallader, Charles, 119
Calcutta (India), 62, 95
Canada, source of free labor tobacco, 61
Canby, Charles, 13 n.
Canton (China), source of free labor sugar, 60, 62
Canton flannel, defined, 88 n.
Cash transactions, found necessary in free produce business, 63; suspended during panic of 1857, 91
Cattell, Ezra, 54

Cavender, John H., 25
Centre, Del., 112
Centreville, Washington Co., Pa., 119
Centreville Abolition Society (Washington Co., Pa.), 20
Chace, Elizabeth (Buffum), 31 n.
Champion of Freedom, prospectus of, 44
Chandler, Elizabeth Margaret, 112 f.
Chandler, Margaret (Evans), 112
Chandler, Thomas, 112
Charles, Henry, 73 f.
Charleston, S. C., 75
Chester Co., Iowa, 119
Chester Co., Pa., anti-slavery center, 20, 117; home of Taylor family, 83; site of G. W. Taylor's cotton mill, 89
Chinese sugar cane, 79. *See* Sorghum cane
Chocolate, produced by free labor, in Santo Domingo, 62
Cincinnati, Ohio, 69, 74; wholesale center for free labor goods, 50 f., 82, 119
Citizen of the World. See Burritt's Citizen of the World
City and County Anti-Slavery Society (Philadelphia), 23
Clark Co., Ohio, anti-slavery center, 19 f., 50, 117
Clarke and Porter, 119
Clarkson, Thomas, 9 f.
Clarkson Anti-Slavery Association of Citizens of Lancaster and Chester Counties, Pennsylvania, 20; issues call for Requited Labor Convention, 23
Clarkson, Hall (Philadelphia), 15, 36
Clegg, Thomas, British cotton manufacturer, 76
Clement, Isaac, 119
Clothier, Caleb, 25
Coffee, produced by free labor, as goal of free produce movement, 60; in Haiti, 61; in Java, 78; in LaGuayra (Venezuela), 78; in Liberia, 95; in Maracaibo (Venezuela), 78; in Santo Domingo, 78; Wilmington Free Produce Society reports, 14
Coffin, Levi, 33, 85, 93, 98, 105; comments on market for free labor goods, 64, 97; complains about quality of free labor goods, 64; conducts free produce store, 51, 82, 119; has cotton gins made, 69 f., 74; officer of Wayne Co. (Ind.) Free Produce Association,

49; seeks free labor cotton, 65, 69
Collins, Charles, 60; conducts free produce store, 81, 119
Collins Center, Erie Co., N. Y., 118; free produce society in, 45; Quakers of, join Progressive Friends, 24 n.
Colonization of Negroes, condemned by Quakers, 30
Colored Female Free Produce Society (Philadelphia), 19, 117
Colored Free Produce Society of Pennsylvania, 18 f., 117
Columbiana County, Ohio, anti-slavery center, 19, 56, 108; market for free labor goods in, 97
Comly, Samuel, purchases free labor cotton, 17
Committee on Manufactures, of Philadelphia Free Produce Association, 85; amount of goods manufactured, 69, 70 f., 73; difficulties of, 69
Committee on Requited Labor, 35
Committee on the Concerns of the People of Color, 33, 48
Compromise of 1850, effect on anti-slavery movement, 38
Connecticut, source of free labor tobacco, 62
Cornish, Samuel E. (Negro), edits *Freedom's Journal*, 111
Cost of free labor goods. *See* Free labor goods
"Cottage gin" introduced, 73 f.
Cotton, produced by free labor, amounts available, 66, 68, 71, 76; amounts obtained, 62, 64, 68, 72; as goal of free produce movement, 60; attempts to create large market for, 70 f., 91, 95; difficulties in ginning, 66 n.; in Alabama, 65, 74; in Illinois, 61 f.; in Louisiana, 72; in Mississippi, 65-68, 70 f., 74; in North Carolina, 17, 60; in Ohio, 61 f.; in Tennessee, 66 f., 71, 74; in Texas, 63, 72; inferior quality of, 64; Pennsylvania Free Produce Society seeks, 15; Philadelphia Free Produce Association purchases, 66, 69, 70; seeks, 37, 65; price of, 62, 67, 69, 70; proof of its free labor origin, 66; sea island variety not produced by free labor, 76; search for outside the United States, 76; shipped to England, 44, 69, 70, 73, 87-89; supply in the United

States, scattered, 61, 76; cut off by Civil War, 91
Cotton cloth, made from free labor cotton, amounts manufactured, 64, 73; by American Free Produce Association, 28; by Charles Collins, 60; by Female Association for Promoting the Manufacture and Use of Free Cotton, 17; by Philadelphia Free Produce Association, 37; complaints about quality of, 64, 71, 85; cost of, 64, 73, 97; difficulties in manufacture of, 69, 85; difficulties in obtaining, 39; first notice of, 13; G. W. Taylor manufactures, 89 f.; G. W. Taylor supplies all, 85; manufactured in England, 86 f.; varieties manufactured, 60, 62, 64, 73, 86-89, 98
Cotton manufacturers, attitude toward using free labor cotton exclusively, 70, 85; free labor cotton handled at small mills only, 73, 85 f.
Cotton market (United States), free produce leaders wish to destroy, 77
Credit transactions, found unsuitable in free produce business, 63; adopted during panic of 1857, 91
Crow, William, a nonslaveholding farmer, 68

Davis, Micajah, 11 n.
Delaine (cloth), defined, 88
Delaware Society for Promoting the Abolition of Slavery, endorses boycott of slave labor goods, 12
Demerara (British Guiana), 79
Depression of 1842, effect on free produce movement in the West, 49 f., on American Free Produce Association, 63
Diggs, Pleasant, nonslaveholding farmer, 68
Disownment of Quakers for anti-slavery views, 31, 104
District Convention of Indiana Abolitionists, 48
Douglass, Frederick, supports free produce cause, 75

Earle, Thomas, 12
East Indian sugar, a product of free labor, 10; tariffs discriminate against, 77 f.

East Indies, source of free labor products, 61 f., 80, 95
Economic aspects of free produce movement, 69 n., 70-72, 114. *See also* Free produce movement
Eddy, Job, cotton manufacturer, 86
Edgerton, Walter, 33 n.
Egypt, source of free labor cotton, 65
Egypt, N. J., 119
Eli & Livezey, 119
Ellis, David, 25
Emancipation, immediate, 30
Emancipation in British colonies, 26, 57, 62
Emancipator (Elihu Embree, ed.), 100 f.
Embree, Elihu, 100 f.
Emery, Moses, 119
Executive Committee of the Eastern District Anti-Slavery Society of Pennsylvania, publishes *Pennsylvania Freeman*, 103

Fairchild, O., and Co., 119
Farmington Quarterly Meeting (Ontario Co., N. Y.), address of published, 53 n.; supports free produce movement, 41
Female Association for Promoting the Manufacture and Use of Free Cotton, declines, 18; organized, 16; purchases and manufactures cotton, 17 f., 61 f.
Female Society for the Relief of British Negro Slaves, 57
Ferrisburgh, Vt., 46 f., 118
Field, Thomas S., and Company, agent for Philadelphia Free Produce Association, 69, 119
Financing of free produce movement. *See* Free produce movement, finances of
Fisher, Joel, conducts free produce store, 81 f., 119
Fisler, Eve, grandmother of G. W. Taylor, 83
"Floats" (in weaving), defined, 96 n.
Florida, source of free labor sugar, 77
Flushing, L. I., Friends' boarding school at, 84
Foster, Abigail (Kelley), 22, 31 n.
Foster, Stephen Symonds, 22 n.; endorses free produce cause, 114
Fourth and Arch Street Meeting (Philadelphia), leader of conservative Friends, 32

Fountain City, Ind., 33. *See* Newport, Ind.
France, source of free labor products, 93
Franklin, Benjamin, 5 n.
Free labor, condition of not noticed, 77 n.; superior to slave labor, 12, 15, 40, 77
Free Labor Advocate and Anti-Slavery Chronicle (Newport, Wayne Co., Ind.; Benjamin Stanton and Henry H. Way, eds.), 32, 49; organ of Anti-Slavery Friends, 33, 104; publicizes free produce movement, 104
Free Labor Association of Maine, 47, 118
Free labor goods, authenticity of questioned, 37, 64, 66, 97; cash transactions necessary in sale of, 63; complaints about quality of, 64, 71, 85, 97-99; demand for, 15-17, 22, 81, 85, 96 f.; difficulties in obtaining, 39, 87; effect of panic of 1842 on, 49 f.; higher price of, 64, 97 f.; manufacture of, 13, 17, 28, 60, 62, 64, 69, 73, 85-87; seasonal market for, 87; supplied to Friends' boarding schools, 38, 63
Free labor products, American Free Produce Association lists sources of, 26 f.; optimism concerning supply of, 18, 77 f.; search for, 15 f., 37, 60-80. *See also* Cotton, Rice, Sugar, Coffee, Indigo, Tobacco, and names of various free produce societies
Free Produce and Anti-Slavery Society of Monroe County, Ohio, 19, 117
Free Produce Association at Collins and Its Vicinity (Erie Co., N. Y.), 45, 118
Free Produce Association of Friends in Ferrisburgh (Vt.) Monthly Meeting, 47
Free Produce Association of Friends of New England Yearly Meeting, 45 f., 59, 118; members sign pledge, 46
Free Produce Association of Friends of New York Yearly Meeting, 46, 59, 75, 78, 117; finances of, 42-44; issues tracts, 43; meetings of, 42-44; organized, 41; sponsors store, 42, 82; supports *Non-Slaveholder*, 44
Free Produce Association of Friends of Ohio Yearly Meeting, 59, 118; auxiliary societies of, 56; contributes articles to Ohio newspapers, 111; finances of, 52, 54 f.; leads in reviving *Non-Slaveholder*, 54 f., 106 f.; organized, 52; plans to publish *Remembrancer*, 54 f.; publishes tracts, 53-56, 106
Free Produce Association of Friends of Philadelphia Yearly Meeting, 36, 59, 64. *See* Philadelphia Free Produce Association
Free Produce Association of Western Vermont, 46, 118
Free produce movement, as a Quaker movement, vii, 59, 115; attempt to make it national in scope, 39, 55; defined, vii; economic aspects of, 69 n., 70-72, 114; finances of, 13, 17, 27, 28, 36, 37, 42, 51, 59, 83, 85, 111; its contribution of Quakerism, 115 f.; numbers engaged in, 14, 36, 53, 56, 115; obscurity of leaders of, vii, 111; propaganda of, 7, 8-10, 15 f., 19, 22, 25-28, 34-38, 43 f., 53-56, 100-113; records of vii, 111; reasons for failure of, 114 f.; summarized, 58, 113-116
Free produce societies, among New York Orthodox Friends, 39-44; among Philadelphia Hicksite Friends, 34 f.; among Philadelphia Orthodox Friends, 35-39; estimated membership of, 110; first one organized, 13; in Great Britain, 57 f.; in Indiana, 48-50; in Iowa, 56 f.; in New England, 45-47; in North Carolina, 47 f.; in Ohio, 19 f., 52-55; in Pennsylvania, 14-19, 23-29, 35-39; in western New York, 44; list of, 117 f.; search for free labor goods is chief work of, 60; summary of, 58 f.
Free Produce Society of Pensylvania, 58, 117; Address to American Convention, 16, 18; expands work, 18; organized, 14; seeks free labor products, 15, 60; sells free labor goods, 62
Free produce stores, 18, 38, 62; find cash transactions necessary, 63; in Baltimore, 81, 119; in Cincinnati, 50 f., 82, 119; in Great Britain, 58; in Indiana, 82, 119; in Iowa, 57, 119; in Mount Pleasant, Ohio, 52, 82, 119; in New Jersey, 81, 119; in New York, 42-44, 62, 81, 82, 92, 119; in Ohio, 52, 71, 82, 97, 119; in Philadelphia, 63, 81-83, 119; in the West, 49, 82,

138 INDEX

97, 119; in Wilmington, Del., 62, 119; list of, 119; numbers of 81 f.; proposals to establish, 24, 26, 37; sources of information concerning, 82 n.; wholesale business of, 81, 82

Freedom's Journal (New York; Samuel E. Cornish and John B. Russwurm, Negroes, eds.), 111; location of file of, 111 n.

Friend, The, G. W. Taylor publishes, 84; liberal Quakers dissatisfied with, 106

Friend of Freedom and Free Labor Advocate (Sodus Bay, N. Y.), 44

Friends, Society of, and Abolition movement, 3 f., 30; attitude toward social reform, 3, 115 f.; conservative faction disapproves of free produce movement, 38, 114; controlled by conservative faction, 31; importance of free produce movement in, 115 f.; radical faction in, 3 f., 31, 114; reforms advocated by, 115

Friends, Society of (Conservative or Wilburite), formed by seceding faction in New England and Ohio, 32

Friends, Society of (Hicksite), activity of in free produce cause, 22 f.; compromise on slavery question in Philadelphia, 34; disown members for anti-slavery views, 31 n.; organize Association of Friends for Promoting the Abolition of Slavery, and Improving the Condition of the Free People of Colour, 34 f.; support free produce movement, in Ohio, 52, in western New York, 44

Friends, Society of (Orthodox), conservative faction disapproves of free produce movement, 32, 39, 102, 104; members form free produce societies, 35, 52. *See also* names of the various yearly meetings

Friends' Bible and Tract Association, G. W. Taylor is agent for, 84

Friends' Intelligencer, 111

Friends' Review (Enoch Lewis, ed.), 39; publicizes free produce movement, 106, 111; represents liberal portion of Quakers, 106

Friends' Preparative Meeting School (Burlington, N. J.), G. W. Taylor teaches at, 84

Fugitive Slave Law (1850), a blow to abolition movement, 56

Garnett, Henry H. (Negro), edits *Impartial Citizen*, 111

Garrett, Edward, 36, 65 n.

Garrison, Wendell Phillips, 102

Garrison, William Lloyd, attends American Free Produce Association meeting, 26; association with Benjamin Lundy, 101; endorses free produce cause, 21, 102, 114; edits *Liberator*, 101 f.; repudiates free produce cause, 21 n., 102, 114

General Anti-Slavery Conventions (London, 1840, 1843), 26, 57

Genius of Universal Emancipation (Benjamin Lundy, ed.), 101; Elizabeth M. Chandler contributes to, 112 f.; location of files of, 13 n.; publicizes free produce movement, 101

Georgia, secession sentiment in, 74 f.

German immigrants, as producers of free labor cotton, 109; as producers of free labor sugar, 74 n., 79 f.

Gibbons, James S., 23 n., 31 n.

Gibbons, William, 13 n.

Gilbert, E. W., 13 n.

Ginger, produced by free labor, in Liberia, 80

Ginning free labor cotton, difficulties encountered in, 66 n.; Nathan Thomas arranges for, 67

Gins (cotton), 5; "cottage gin" introduced, 73; owned chiefly by slaveholders, 66; owned by nonslaveholding farmers, 73; rented by nonslaveholding farmers, 70; supplied to nonslaveholding farmers, 67, 70

Goddell, William, remarks on free produce cause, 25 n.

Grant County, Ind., 119

Grave, Jacob, 49

Great Britain, 93; anti-slavery societies in, 57; emancipation in colonies of, 26, 57; free labor cotton manufactured in, 86 f.; free produce movement in, 43, 57 f.; sugar boycotted in, 9 f.

Green Plain, Clark Co., Ohio, 119; anti-slavery center, 19 f.; Western Free Produce convention at, 50

Green Plain Free Produce Society (Clark Co., Ohio), 19 f., 117
Green Plain Quarterly Meeting (Hicksite) (Clark Co., Ohio), joins Progressive Friends, 24 n.
Greeneville, Tenn., 101
Greensboro, Henry Co., Ind., free produce store in, 63 n., 119; Western Free Produce Convention at, 50
Grew, Henry, 25
Grey, William & Co., 119
Griffitts, Samuel Powell, 11 n.
Guilford County, N. C., 118; source of free labor cotton, 17 f., 61
Gunn, Lewis C., 25; publishes *Address to Abolitionists*, 25 f.
Gurney, Joseph John, 114; and doctrinal controversy, 32, 105

Haiti, source of free labor products, 60 f.
Hallowell, William S., 14
Hallowell, Me., 119
Hambleton, Alice Eliza, 25
Hampton, Martha, 25
Harrison County, Ohio, 20, 117
Harrisville Free Produce and Anti-Slavery Society (Harrison Co., Ohio), 20, 117
Haverford College, Haverford, Pa., 38 n.
Hawaii, source of free labor products, 63 n., 78, 78 n.
Herald of Freedom (Wilmington, Ohio), location of file of, 111 n.; publicizes free produce movement, 111
Hicks, Elias, condemns use of slave labor goods, 7 f.; doctrinal controversy, 7 n.
Hicksite Friends. *See* Friends, Society of (Hicksite)
Hilles, Eli, 13 n.
Hinshaw, Seth, conducts free produce store, 63 n., 119
Hoag, Lindley Murray, conducts free produce store, 42, 82, 119
Hodgson, Adam, writes letter on free and slave labor costs, 12
Holland, source of free labor sugar, 93
Holly Springs, Miss., Nathan Thomas visits, 66
Hopper, Isaac Tatem, 14, 15 n.; disowned, 23 n., 31 n.; publishes *National Anti-Slavery Standard*, 110
Horn, John, 6 f.

Hostility of the South, resulting from slavery question, 68, 74 f.
Hunt, J. Anderson, nonslaveholding farmer, 68; hires a slave, 74; receives cotton gin, 70 f.
Hunt, Nathan, Jr., supplies free labor cotton, 17 f., 61
Hunt, R. S., nonslaveholding farmer, 68

Illinois, source of free labor cotton, 61 f.
Imlay, Gilbert, predicts use of maple sugar, 10
Impartial Citizen (Syracuse, N. Y.; Henry H. Garnett, Negro, ed.), 111
Imphee (sorghum cane), 80
India, "cottage gin" used in, 73; slavery in, 20; source of free labor products, 63, 76, 78; sugar production hampered by tariffs, 77
Indiana, 100; free produce movement in, 48-50, 115
Indiana Yearly Meeting of Anti-Slavery Friends (Orthodox), 49, 105; adopts free labor principle, 34; arranges free produce conventions, 50; *Free Labor Advocate* reflects views of, 104; organized, 33
Indiana Yearly Meeting (Hicksite), "lays down" Green Plain Quarterly Meeting, 24 n.
Indiana Yearly Meeting (Orthodox), acknowledges error, 33 f.; Committee on the Concerns of the People of Color of, 33, 48; dissension between radicals and conservatives, 32, 49, 104; secession of radical faction, 33
Indigo, produced by free labor, 63 n.
Inglis, Bessie, conducts free produce store, 58
Iowa, free produce movement in, 56 f., 97, 118, 119
Iowa Free Produce Association, 118
Isle of Wight County, Va., source of free labor products, 80

Jaffrey, N. H., resident of attempts to make sugar from potatoes, 78
Java, source of free labor products, 60, 62, 78
Jefferson, Thomas, plants maple trees, 11
Jenkins, George K., 107 n.
Johnson, Israel H., 36, 65 n.
Johnson, William H., 25

Index

Jonesboro, Ind., 119
Jonesboro, Tenn., 100

Kaolin, Chester Co., Pa., 83
Kelley, Abigail. *See* Foster, Abigail (Kelley)
Kennett Square, Chester Co., Pa., 119; center of Progressive Friends, 23 n.
Kentucky, source of free labor tobacco, 62
Kenworthy, Jesse, 20
Kesley, William, 16
Koloa Plantation, Hawaii, 78 n.
Krafft, John H., Memphis cotton factor, 66 f., 72

Lafayette County, Miss., 67
La Guayra (Venezuela), source of free labor products, 60, 63 n., 78
Laing, A., 119
Lamb, Michael, opens free produce store, 81, 119
Lay, Benjamin, 5
Leech, Thomas, and Company, cotton factors, 67, 91
Levering, Griffith, organizes Alum Creek Free Produce Association, 56
Lewis, Alice (Jackson), 6
Lewis, Enoch, 6; attends North Carolina Yearly Meeting, 47; author of free produce tract, 53 n.; edits *Friends' Review*, 106; officer of Philadelphia Free Produce Association, 36; teacher, 83 f.
Lewis, Sidney Ann, 25, 119
Liberator (W. L. Garrison, ed.), 101; publicizes free produce movement, 101
Liberia, source of free labor products, 76, 80, 94 f.
Lindley, C. K., 48
Little Rock, Ark., 72
Liverpool, free labor cotton shipped to, 70, 73, 87
London (England), 83; center of free produce movement, 58
London Yearly Meeting, discusses free produce cause, 57 f.; sends mission to reconcile factions of Indiana Yearly Meeting, 33
Louisiana, source of free labor products, 72, 78 f.; sugar production protected, 80
Lundy, Benjamin, 21, 77; addresses Colored Free Produce Society, 19; first to seek free labor products, 60 f.; founds Anti-Slavery Society of Maryland, 12 n.; in American Convention, 12, 16; journalistic work of, 100 f., 112; opens free produce store, 81, 119; visits Texas, 101
Lynn, Mass., free produce stores in, 81, 119

Mabbett, le. *See* Mabbett, Lorenzo
Mabbett, Lorenzo, 44 f.; author of free produce tract, 53 n.
McClintock, Thomas, 14, 15 n.
McClure, Robert, 119
McKim, James Miller, 63; edits *Pennsylvania Freeman*, 103 f.
McRay, William, nonslaveholding farmer, 68, 74; promises to supply free labor cotton, 70
Macy, Jonathan, 119
Maine, free produce movement in, 47, 97
Managers. *See* Board of Managers
Manchester (England), free produce store in, 58; manufacture of free labor cotton in, 58
Manchester, Me., 47, 118
Manila, Philippine Islands, source of free labor products, 63 n., 78
Manufacture of free labor cotton. *See* Cotton cloth, made from free labor cotton; Mill, to manufacture free labor cotton
Manufacturers. *See* Cotton manufacturers
Manufacturing Committee. *See* Committee on Manufactures
Manumission societies, 30
Maple sugar, 62; increase in production of, 80; only sugar produced by free labor in United States, 61; substitute for slave-grown cane sugar, 10, 78
Maracaibo (Venezuela), source of free labor products, 78
Marion County (Ohio) Free Produce Association, 48, 117
Marriott, Charles, advocates free produce cause, 22, 23 n.; disowned, 31 n.
Marshall County, Miss., source of free labor cotton, 68
Maryland Anti-Slavery Society. *See* Anti-Slavery Society of Maryland
Meeting for Sufferings, action in Indiana Yearly Meeting, 32; defined, 31 n.;

Index

supports free produce movement in New York, 41
Meetinghouses (Quaker), closed to abolitionists, 31; closed to free produce societies, 31, 38
Memphis (Tenn.) cotton market, 66, 71-73
Methodist Episcopal Church, 3, 30
Mexican War, Quakers' view of, 38
Mexico, source of free labor products, 77 f.
Michigan (Territory), 112
Mifflin, Warner, 6, 12
Miles, Henry, 46 n., 55; contributes articles to *Vergennes* (Vt.) *Citizen*, 111; organizes free produce societies in Vermont, 46; promotes national free produce movement, 39, 46; seeks free labor products, 80
Mill, to manufacture free labor cotton, G. W. Taylor operates, 89-91, 96; proposed, 39, 56
Miller, Daniel L., Jr., 25, 64; buys free labor cotton, 67
Miller, Samuel, 11 n.
Mississippi, source of free labor cotton, 65-68, 70, 71, 74
Missouri Compromise, 100 f.
Mobile, Ala., 74
Molasses, from free labor sources, attempt to make it from potatoes, 78; Charles Pierce sells, 62; made from sorghum cane, 79 f.; Pennsylvania Free Produce Society seeks, 15
Monroe County, Ohio, anti-slavery center, 19, 117
Monthly meetings, 31 n.
Morris, Thomas, 50
Morrow County, Ohio, free produce movement in, 50 n., 56, 97, 118
Morton, R., 75
Moses Brown School, Providence, R. I., 38 n.
Mott, James, 14, 15 n., 119
Mott, Lucretia, 25, 31 n., 99
Mount Pleasant, Ohio, anti-slavery center, 52, 100, 118; free produce store at, 52, 119
Mount Pleasant Free Produce Company, operates a store, 82, 119; organized, 52; records of, 56
Murfreesboro, N. C., source of free labor cotton, 60

Murray, Robert Lindley, conducts free produce store, 42 f., 82, 119; ships cotton to England, 73, 87; supplies free labor sugar, 92-94

Nansemond County, Va., source of free labor products, 80
National Anti-Slavery Standard (New York), publicizes free produce movement, 110
National Enquirer and Constitutional Advocate of Universal Liberty (Philadelphia; Benjamin Lundy, ed.), location of files of, 103 n.; publicizes free produce movement, 103
Negroes, colonization of condemned by Quakers, 30; condition of, in British West Indies, 57 n., 73; edit anti-slavery papers, 110; "murdered" by consumers of slave labor products, 10; raise tobacco in Canada, 61
New Bedford, Mass., 86
New England, Benjamin Lundy visits, 101; free produce societies in, 45-47, 115; Wilbur-Gurney controversy in, 32
New Garden, Pa., 83
New Garden Anti-Slavery Society (Columbiana Co., Ohio), 19
New Garden Quarterly Meeting (Guilford Co., N. C.), supports free produce cause, 48
New Garden Quarterly Meeting (Wayne Co., Ind.), supports free produce cause, 48
New Hampshire, resident of attempts to make sugar from potatoes, 78
New Jersey, free produce stores in, 81, 119
New Orleans (La.), Nathan Thomas visits, 72, 74
New York (state), free produce movement in, 41-44, 115; free produce stores in, 81, 119
New York City, 78, 85, 92, 117, 119; free produce stores in, 42-44, 62
New York Manumission Society, republishes Adam Hodgson's letter, 12
New York Yearly Meeting (Orthodox), attitude toward free produce movement, 40 f.; members form free produce society, 41-44

INDEX

Newcastle-on-Tyne (England), anti-slavery press at, 109 f.; free produce movement in, 58
Newport, Jesse W., 16
Newport, R. I., 118
Newport, Wayne Co., Ind., anti-slavery convention held at, 49; center of Anti-Slavery Friends, 33, 104; free produce stores in, 63 n., 119; *Free Labor Advocate* published at, 104; *Protectionist* published at, 104
Nine Partners School (Schenectady, N. Y.), 38 n.
Non-Slaveholder (Philadelphia), 38, 39, 42, 45, 56; avoids doctrinal issues, 105; ceases publication, 106; is revived, 54 f., 107 f.; location of files of, 108 n.; publicizes free produce movement, 105, 108; reception among Friends generally, 105; succeeded by *Burritt's Citizen of the World*, 108
Nonslaveholding farmers in the South, competition with slave labor, 69 n., 72; free produce societies desire to aid them, 15, 72; source of free labor cotton, 15, 17, 37, 60-62, 65, 68, 70-72
North American Free Labor Produce Association, 40, 46, 109, 118
North Carolina, source of free labor products, 17, 18, 60, 62 f., 65, 80
North Carolina Free Produce Association, 47, 118; effect of Compromise of 1850 on, 47 f.

Oberlin College (Oberlin, Ohio), free produce movement at, 55
Oberlin Evangelist (Ohio), location of file of, 111 n.; publicizes free produce movement, 111
"Oh Press Me Not to Taste Again" (poem), 113
Ohio, 101; free produce movement in, 19 f., 52-56, 115; free produce stores in, 50-52, 82, 119; G. W. Taylor visits, 84; Wilbur-Gurney controversy in, 32
Ohio Anti-Slavery Society, 19
Ohio Columbian (Columbus), location of file of, 111; publicizes free produce movement, 111
Ohio Free Produce Association. *See* Free Produce Association of Friends of Ohio Yearly Meeting

Ohio Yearly Meeting (Hicksite), approves free produce movement, 52
Ohio Yearly Meeting (Orthodox), approves free produce cause, 56; members form free produce society, 52 f.
Orthodox Friends. *See* Friends, Society of (Orthodox)
Osborn, Charles, vii; edits *Philanthropist*, 100; removed from Meeting for Sufferings, 32
Oxford Free Produce Society (Chester Co., Pa.), 20, 22. *See also* Union Free Produce Society

Palmer, Jonathan, Jr., 14
Palmer, Norris W., 119
Park, J., 119
Parker, Joel, conducts free produce store, 63 n., 93, 119
Parker, Joseph, 14, 16
Parrish, Joseph, 14, 15 n., 16
Peirce, Isaac, 13 n., 119
Pennock, Abraham L., edits *Non-Slaveholder*, 105; officer of free produce societies, 14, 25, 36, 65 n.
Pennock, Amy, 119
Pennsylvania, 84; Executive Committee of the Eastern District Anti-Slavery Society of Pennsylvania publishes *Pennsylvania Freeman*, 103; free produce movement in, 14-19, 23-29, 35-39, 115
Pennsylvania Freeman (Philadelphia), 110; John Greenleaf Whittier edits, 103; J. Miller McKim edits, 103 f.; location of files of, 104 n.; publicizes free produce movement, 103
Pennsylvania Hall (Philadelphia), 23; burning of, 24
Pennsylvania Society for Promoting the Abolition of Slavery, for the Relief of Free Negroes Unlawfully Held in Bondage, and for Improving the Condition of the African Race, 15 n.; endorses free produce idea, 16; refuses to participate in Requited Labor Convention, 24
Pennsylvania Yearly Meeting of Progressive Friends, origin, 23. *See also* Progressive Friends
Pepper, produced by free labor, in Liberia, 95
Percival, B., 119

Permanent Board, defined, 31 n.
Perquimans County, N. C., source of free labor products, 80
Peterson, George, 14
Philadelphia, 112, 117, 119; anti-slavery societies in, 23 f.; free produce societies in, 14-19, 23-29, 35-39, 115; free produce stores in, 63, 81, 83, 119; panic of 1857 in, 91
Philadelphia City Anti-Slavery Society, 23
Philadelphia Female Anti-Slavery Society, 27 f.
Philadelphia Free Produce Association of Friends, 57, 98, 118; amounts of cotton purchased, 68, 70, 73; attempts to create large market for free labor cotton, 70, 71, 95; cost of cotton purchased, 67, 69, 70, 73; effect of Compromise of 1850 on, 38; employs agent to seek free labor cotton, 37, 65 f., 71; finances of, 69-71, 73, 85; investigates free labor character of Puerto Rican sugar, 79; manufactures cotton cloth, 69, 70 f., 73; meetings of, 37-40; organized, 36; purchases free labor cotton, 66, 69, 70; purposes of, 64 f.; seeks free labor products, 65, 97; sells goods to Levi Coffin, 51; ships cotton to England, 70; transfers goods to G. W. Taylor, 38, 73; value of goods in 1848, 73. *See also* Board of Managers, Committee on Manufactures
Philadelphia Yearly Meeting (Hicksite), members form Association of Friends for Promoting the Abolition of Slavery and Improving the Condition of the Free People of Colour, 34 f.
Philadelphia Yearly Meeting (Orthodox), 36 f.; conservative faction disapproves of free produce movement, 38, 40, 105; influence of Wilbur-Gurney controversy on, 32, 105; members form free produce society, 36; "Minute on Slavery" of, 40 n.
Philadelphia Yearly Meeting of Women Friends, 6
Philanthropist (Mount Pleasant, Ohio; Charles Osborn, ed.), 100
Philippine Islands, source of free labor products, 63 n., 78
Pickering, Elihu, 36, 65 n.

Pierce, Charles, 80; amount of goods sold by, 62, 78; conducts free produce store, 18, 81, 119
Pierce, James L., conducts free produce store, 81, 119
"Plain dress," G. W. Taylor adopts, 84; Quaker testimony, 86
"Plain language," G. W. Taylor uses, 84
Political aspects of abolition movement, 30
Poole, William, 11 n.
Potatoes, attempt to make sugar from, 78
Premiums, offered for free labor products, 19, 21 n., 61, 80
Presbyterian church, 3
Printing cloth, defined, 86 n.
Prize goods, defined, 100 n.; synonymous with slave labor goods, 4, 7
Progressive Friends, 23 n., 33 n., 114
Propaganda of the free produce movement, 7, 8-10, 15 f., 19, 22, 25-28, 34-38, 43 f., 53-56, 100-113
Protectionist (Newport, Wayne Co., Ind.; Arnold Buffum, ed.), 104; location of file of, 104 n.
Puerto Rico, free labor character of products questioned, 78; source of free labor products, 18, 62, 78
Pugh, Sarah, 25
Pusey, Lea, 13 n.

Quakers, attitude toward slavery, 3 f.; free produce movement associated with, 21, 59; support manumission societies, 30. *See also* Friends, Society of
Quality of free labor goods, complaints about, 64, 71, 85, 97-99
Quarterly meetings, 31 n.

Radnor, Pa., 83
Rahway, N. J., 119
Rawle, William, 14
Remembrancer, 107
Requited Labor Convention, 23-25; forms American Free Produce Association, 24; reported in *Pennsylvania Freeman*, 103; societies represented in, 24 n.
Reynolds, John, 13 n.
Rhoads, Samuel, edits *Non-Slaveholder*, 105, 107; officer of Philadelphia Free Produce Association, 36, 65 n.; publishes tract on free produce, 35 f.; trustee of free produce funds, 96

INDEX

Rhode Island, 38 n., 81, 104; free produce movement in, 45 f.

Rice, produced by free labor, as goal of free produce movement, 60; G. W. Taylor obtains, 95; in East Indies, 18 n., 80, 95; in Liberia, 80; in North Carolina, 18, 80; in Virginia, 80; Pennsylvania Free Produce Society seeks, 15; Philadelphia Free Produce Association seeks, 37, 72, 74 n.; scarcity of, in United States, 61

Richards, David, grandfather of G. W. Taylor, 83

Richards, Elizabeth (Megee), grandmother of G. W. Taylor, 83

Richards, William P., 13 n.

Richardson, Anna H., edits *The Slave*, 109

Richardson, Richard, trustee of free produce funds, 96

Richmond, Ind., free labor cotton spun at, 61

Rochester, N. Y., 75

Rogers, William, 11 n.

Rowland, Joseph G., 13 n.

Rush, Benjamin, advocates use of maple sugar, 10

Russell, Henry, 119

Russwurm, John B. (Negro), edits *Freedom's Journal*, 111

Saco, Me., 119

St. Croix (West Indies), source of free labor sugar, 79, 94

St. Lucia (West Indies), source of free labor sugar, 92

St. Thomas (West Indies), G. W. Taylor visits, 79

Salem, Columbiana Co., Ohio, anti-slavery center, 19, 56; supports *Non-Slavholder*, 108

Salem (Columbiana Co., Ohio) Abolition and Colonization Society, 19

Salem, Henry Co., Iowa, anti-slavery center, 56 f., 118

Salem, Union Co., Ind., free produce movement in, 50 f.

Sampson, Alden, 119

Sandiford, Ralph, 4 f.

Sandwich, Mass., 119

Sandwich Islands. *See* Hawaii

Santo Domingo, source of free labor products, 60, 62, 63 n., 78

Savannah, Ga., 75

Say, Jean-Baptiste, letter to, on slave and free labor costs, 12

Scarlet, C. M. & M. J., 119

Scholfield, David, 16

Scipio Quarterly Meeting (Cayuga Co., N. Y.), supports free produce movement, 40

Shipley, Thomas, 14, 15 n., 16

Shoemaker, Nathan, 14

Slave, The; His Wrongs and Their Remedy (Newcastle-on-Tyne, England), 58; Elihu Burritt edits, 109; location of file of, 109 n.

Slave labor, compared with free labor, 12, 15, 40; competition with white labor in the South, 69 n., 72; purpose of free produce movement to make it unprofitable, 77

Slave labor goods, abolitionists claim special right to use, 102, 114; use of condemned by William Allen, 8; by American Anti-Slavery Society, 21; by American Convention, 11 f.; by American Free Produce Association, 24; by Anti-Slavery Convention of American Women, 22; by Thomas Branagan, 8 f.; by British public, 9 f.; by Delaware and Maryland Anti-Slavery Societies, 12; by Female Association for Promoting the Manufacture and Use of Free Cotton, 16 f.; by Free Produce Society of Pennsylvania, 16; by W. L. Garrison, 21, 102; by Elias Hicks, 7; by John Horn, 6 f.; by Indiana Yearly Meeting of Anti-Slavery Friends, 34; by Benjamin Lay, 5; by Alice (Jackson) Lewis, 6; by Benjamin Lundy, 12 f.; by Charles Marriott, 22; by Warner Mifflin, 6; by Requited Labor Convention, 24; by Samuel Rhoads, 35; by Union Free Produce Society, 20; by John Woolman, 4-6

"Slave Produce" (poem), 113

Slave trade, 4; British attempt to abolish (1791), 9 f.

Slavery, 3; as a national issue, 74; in British colonies, 26, 57; in India, 20; in Venezuela, 60 n.; in West Indies, 4, 6, 10; opposition to after American Revolution, 10

Index

145

Slaves, "murdered" by consumers of slave labor products, 10; paid for ginning cotton, 66 n.
Small, Coleman & Co., 119
Small, John, 72
Small, S., 119
Smith, Elihu Hubbard, 11 n.
Smith, Gerrit, vii, 25; endorses free produce cause, 114; gives money to Philadelphia Free Produce Association, 69 n.
Smith, Samuel, 14
Sorghum cane and molasses, 79 f.
South, the, agitated by slavery question, 74 f.; reaction to free produce movement, 68, 74 f.; source of free labor cotton, 65-68, 70-74
South Africa, source of free labor cotton, 76
South America, source of free labor products, 61, 76
South Carolina, secession sentiment in, 74 f.; source of free labor cotton, 18, 62
Southampton County, Va., source of free labor products, 80
Southwick, Thankful, 22
Spiceland, Ind., anti-slavery convention held at, 49
Spices, produced by free labor, 95
Staines (England), 83
Stanton, Benjamin, edits *Free Labor Advocate*, 104; officer of Wayne County Free Produce Association, 49; removed from Meeting for Sufferings, 32
Stanton, Henry B., 30
Stanton, Nathan, operates free produce store, 75, 119
Starr, C. W., spins free labor cotton, 61
Stores. See Free produce stores
Stowe, Calvin Ellis, addresses free produce meeting, 58; endorses free produce movement, 89, 110
Stowe, Harriet Beecher, vii; addresses free produce meeting, 58; endorses free produce movement, 89, 110
Stuart, R. L. & A., sugar refiners, 92
Sturge, Joseph, 57; gives money to Philadelphia Free Produce Association, 71
Sugar, attempt to make it from potatoes, 78; grades of, 92 f.; price of, 94; production in Louisiana protected, 80; tariffs on, 77, 93. See also West Indian sugar, East Indian sugar

Sugar, maple. See Maple sugar
Sugar, produced by free labor, as goal of free produce movement, 60; difficulties in procuring, 77 f.; G. W. Taylor's trade in, 92-94; in East Indies, 10, 77 f.; in Hawaii, 78; in India, 77; in LaGuayra (Venezuela), 78, 92; in Mexico, 77, 78; in Philippine Islands, 78, 92; in Puerto Rico, 78 f.; in St. Croix, 79, 94; in St. Lucia, 92; in St. Thomas, 79; in West Indies, 61 f., 76, 77-79; Nathan Thomas seeks, 74; Pennsylvania Free Produce Society seeks, 15, 18; Philadelphia Free Produce Association seeks, 37; scarcity of, in United States, 61
"Sugar-Plums, The" (poem), 113
Suspicion as to authenticity of free labor products, 37, 64, 66, 97. See also Free labor goods
Syracuse, N. Y., 111

Taber, Louis, author of free produce tract, 53 n.
Taft, Levi, 44
Tallahatchie River, 67
Tappan, Lewis, 25
Tatham, Benjamin, 75
Taylor, Elizabeth (Burton), third wife of G. W. Taylor, 84
Taylor, Elizabeth (Richards), mother of G. W. Taylor, 83
Taylor, Elizabeth (Sykes), first wife of G. W. Taylor, 84
Taylor, Francis, grandfather of G. W Taylor, 83
Taylor, George Washington, 57, 75; biography, 83 f.; conducts free produce store, 82, 83, 92, 97, 119; difficulties in free produce business, 87 f., 98; edits *Non-Slaveholder*, 105-107; effect of panic of 1857 on, 91, 96; financial difficulties of, 83, 85, 87, 89, 95 f.; has cloth manufactured in England, 86 f.; investigates free labor character of Puerto Rican sugar, 79; mail order business of, 85, 97; manufacturing difficulties of, 85 f., 87; officer of Philadelphia Free Produce Association, 36, 65 n., 85; operates cotton mill, 89-91, 96, 98 f.; proposes to establish cotton mill, 39, 89; purchases business location, 85; relations with em-

ployees, 91, 96; publishes *Burritt's Citizen of the World*, 108; rice trade, 95; ships cotton to England, 88; sugar trade, 92-94; supplies all free labor goods, 85; takes over business of Philadelphia Free Produce Association, 38, 73; visits West Indies, 79 f., 85

Taylor, Jacob, father of G. W. Taylor, 83

Taylor, Mary, great-grandmother of G. W. Taylor, 83

Taylor, Richard, great-grandfather of G. W. Taylor, 83

Taylor, Ruth (Leeds), second wife of G. W. Taylor, 84

Temperance movement, 30, 115

Tennessee, 101; source of free labor cotton, 65, 71, 74

Texas, Benjamin Lundy visits, 101; Nathan Thomas visits, 72; source of free labor products, 63, 72, 76, 78 f., 109

Thacker, Dr., an unwilling slaveholder, 70

Thomas, Nathan, 76; comments on secession sentiment in Georgia, 74; comments on Southern people, 69 n.; death of, 75, 76 n.; estate of, 75 n.; extracts from his letters published, 53 n.; how received in the South, 68, 74 f.; remuneration as agent, 68, 72 n.; reports as agent for Philadelphia Free Produce Association, 68, 75; seeks free labor cotton in the South, 65, 71-74; seeks free labor sugar, 74, 78 f; visits Philadelphia, 75

Thomas, Zebulon, 119

Tobacco, produced by free labor, in Canada, 61; in Connecticut, 62; in Kentucky, 62; in Ohio, 61; Pennsylvania Free Produce Society seeks, 15

Towne, Ezra, 92; conducts free produce store, 43, 82, 119

Townsend, John, 119

Townsend, Joseph, 11 n.

Trinidad, 79

Tropical Free Labor Company, 57

Truman, George, 119

Tucker, Benjamin, 14, 15 n.

Twelfth Street Meeting (Philadelphia), leader in free produce movement, 32

Underground Railroad, 33, 107 n.

Union County, Indiana, free produce movement in, 49

Union Free Produce Society (Chester Co., Pa.), 20, 117

Unthank, Jonathan, 49

Venezuela, slavery in, 60 n.; source of free labor products, 60, 63 n., 78

Vergennes (Vt.) *Citizen*, Henry Miles contributes to, 111; location of file of, 111 n.

Vermont, 81; free produce movement in, 46

Virginia, source of free labor products, 46, 80

Ward, Sir Henry G., envoy to Mexico, 77

Washington, N. C., source of free labor cotton and rice, 18

Way, Henry H., edits *Free Labor Advocate*, 104; officer of Wayne County (Ind.) Free Produce Association, 49; removed from Meeting for Sufferings, 32; reorganizes Western Free Produce Association, 51

Way, Moorman, 65

Wayne County, Ind., free produce movement in, 48 f., 117

Wayne County (Ind.) Free Produce Association, 49, 117

Wayne County, N. Y., free produce movement in, 44 f., 117

Wealth of Nations (a projected periodical), 109

Webb, Benjamin, 13 n.

Webb, Jane, 119

Webster, Henry, manager of G. W. Taylor's cotton mill, 89, 96

Weld, Theodore Dwight, 30; boycotts slave labor goods, 21, 114

West, the, free produce movement in, 48-57, 59, 104, 115; market for free labor goods in, 64, 71, 97 f.

West Chester Recorder (Pa.), 100

West Indian sugar, boycotted in Great Britain (1791), 9 f.; emancipation makes it a free labor product, 61, 78 f.; protected by tariff, 77; to be replaced by maple sugar, 10; use of condemned, 6-8

INDEX

West Indies, condition of Negroes in, 57 n., 73; emancipation in, 62; slavery in, 4, 6, 10; source of free labor products, 61 f., 76, 77, 79

Westbury Quarterly Meeting (N. Y.), 44

Western Free Produce Association (Ohio and Ind.), 59, 117; annual meetings, 50; finances, 51; organized, 49; records of, 52; reorganized, 51

Western Manufacturing Company, 51

Western New York Free Produce Association, 44, 117

Westtown School, Westtown, Pa., 38 n.; G. W. Taylor teaches at, 84

Whetstone, Marion Co., Ohio, 48, 117

Whipper, William, 119

White, George F., disowned, 31 n.

White, Lydia, 25, 63; conducts free produce store, 81, 119

Whittier, John Greenleaf, vii; edits *Pennsylvania Freeman*, 103, 112; endorses free produce cause, 112, 114

Wilbur, John, and doctrinal controversy, 32

Wilbur-Gurney controversy, 32; effect on Ohio Free Produce Association, 52

Wilburite Friends. *See* Friends, Society of (Conservative or Wilburite)

Williamson, Francis, 60

Wilmington, Del., free produce movement in, 13 f., 117; free produce stores in, 62, 119

Wilmington (Del.) Society for the Encouragement of Free Labor, 117; action in American Convention, 16, 60; organized, 13; seeks free labor products, 13 f.

Wingrave, John, British cotton manufacturer, 88

Wise, Charles, 64; conducts free produce store, 81, 82 n., 119

Wistar, Caspar, 11 n.

Wistar, Thomas, Jr., 36, 65 n.

Women, appealed to in promoting free produce cause, 17, 21, 112 f. *See also* Anti-Slavery Convention of American Women

Women's rights movement, 3, 22 n., 30

Wood, George, conducts free produce store, 42, 82, 119

Woodward, ———, 119

Woolman, John, 35; condemns use of slave labor goods, 4-6

World Anti-Slavery Conventions. *See* General Anti-Slavery Conventions

Yalobusha County, Miss., source of free labor cotton, 70

Yearly meeting of Friends, as unit of organization, 31 n.

Zollickoffer, Henry M., 14